Rust Programming Language for Web Development

Building High-Performance Web Applications and APIs

Jeff Stuart

Discover Other Books in the Series

"Rust Programming Language for Beginners: The Ultimate Beginner's Guide to Safe and Fast Programming"

"Rust Programming Language for Operating Systems: Build Secure and High-Performance Operating Systems in Rust"

"Rust Programming language for Network: Build Fast, Secure, and Scalable Systems"

"Rust Programming Language for Web Assembly: Build Blazing-Fast, Next-Gen Web Applications"

"Rust Programming Language for Blockchains: Build Secure, Scalable, and High-Performance Distributed Systems"

"Rust Programming Language for Cybersecurity: Writing Secure Code to Implementing Advanced Cryptographic Solutions"

"Rust Programming Language for IoT: The Complete Guide to Developing Secure and Efficient Smart Devices"

"Rust programming Language for Artificial Intelligence: High-performance machine learning with unmatched speed, memory safety, and concurrency from AI innovation"

Disclaimer

The information provided in *"Rust Programming Language for Web Development: Building High-Performance Web Applications and APIs"* by **Jeff Stuart** is intended solely for educational and informational purposes.

Readers are encouraged to consult qualified professionals or official documentation for specific technical, legal, or professional guidance related to their projects.

Introduction

Welcome to "**Rust Programming Language for Web Development**: Building High-Performance Web Applications and APIs." In today's rapidly changing digital environment, where performance, security, and reliability are of utmost importance, selecting the appropriate programming language for your web applications is crucial. Rust stands out as an excellent option, offering a distinctive blend of speed, safety, and concurrency, making it an attractive choice for web developers eager to explore new possibilities.

The ascent of Rust has been truly impressive. Originally intended for system-level programming, it has evolved beyond its initial purpose to serve as a practical solution for web development. Its focus on memory safety and thread safety establishes Rust as a strong alternative to conventional languages in the web sector, where developers frequently encounter performance issues and security threats. Adopting Rust not only boosts the efficiency of your applications but also reduces the risks linked to memory-related errors and concurrent operations.

In this book, we will embark on an exploration of the essential features and capabilities of Rust in the context of web development. We will address the fundamentals— from grasping the language's syntax and principles to delving into its powerful frameworks and libraries tailored for constructing web applications and APIs. You will discover how to develop secure, rapid, and scalable back-end services while effectively leveraging Rust's innovative techniques for data management, asynchronous programming, and more.Whether you are an experienced developer looking to expand your skill set or a newcomer eager to dive into web development, this book is crafted to cater to all levels of expertise. We aim to provide practical insights and hands-on examples to ensure that you can immediately apply what you've learned. As you progress through the chapters, you will build real-world applications and APIs that harness the full potential of Rust, empowering you to develop high-performance solutions that stand out in today's competitive environment.

Learning a new programming language can be a daunting task, but the benefits Rust offers make it a worthwhile endeavor. By the end of this book, you will not only understand the Rust language but also appreciate its capabilities for building modern web applications. Get ready to unlock the power of Rust and embark on a journey that will elevate your web development skills and introduce you to a vibrant community of like-minded developers passionate about pushing the boundaries of technology.

Chapter 1: Introduction to Rust for Web Development

Initially created for systems programming, Rust has progressively expanded into various fields, including web development. This chapter intends to examine the essential principles of Rust and its relevance to web development, offering a summary of its features, benefits, and a comparison with more conventional web development languages.

1.1 What is Rust?

Rust is a statically typed, compiled programming language that prioritizes performance and safety, especially in concurrent programming scenarios. Originating from Mozilla Research and first introduced in 2010, Rust's architecture promotes the creation of efficient and dependable code while mitigating common programming pitfalls such as data races and null pointer dereferences. The language ensures memory safety without relying on a garbage collector, rendering it suitable for environments where performance is paramount.

The fundamental concept of Rust is its ownership model, which imposes stringent regulations on memory access and deallocation. This model allows developers to handle memory in a safe and efficient manner, making Rust an attractive option for web developers focused on building high-performance applications.## 1.2 The Rise of Rust in Web Development

While Rust's applications have predominantly been in systems programming, its rise in the web development sphere can be attributed to several factors:

Performance: Rust's performance is comparable to that of C and C++. This makes it ideal for backend services that handle high traffic and require fast execution times.

Safety: Rust's ownership model provides compile-time checks that prevent many common types of bugs, increasing the reliability of web applications.

Concurrency: Rust's design makes handling concurrent operations more straightforward, an essential aspect of modern web applications that often need to manage multiple incoming requests simultaneously.

WebAssembly (Wasm): The growing popularity of WebAssembly has opened up new avenues for Rust in web development. Wasm enables developers to run code written in languages like Rust in the browser at near-native speed, expanding the potential for high-performance web applications.

1.3 The Rust Ecosystem for Web Development

Rust boasts a rich ecosystem that caters to various aspects of web development. Some of the most notable tools and crates (Rust libraries) include:

Rocket: A web framework that makes it easy to write fast and secure web applications. Its type safety and intuitive API allow developers to build APIs quickly.

Actix: A powerful actor-based framework that is designed to handle asynchronous web applications with a focus on speed and scalability.

Warp: A lightweight and flexible framework that utilizes the async/await syntax for building non-blocking web servers, ideal for modern web applications.

yew: A framework for building client-side web applications with Rust, allowing developers to write single-page applications (SPAs) using Rust and compile them to WebAssembly.

These frameworks, along with various libraries for database interaction, authentication, and templating, form a robust ecosystem for developing web applications in Rust.

1.4 Comparing Rust to Traditional Web Development Languages

When considering Rust for web development, it is essential to contextualize it alongside traditional web development languages like JavaScript, Python, and Ruby. Each language has its strengths and weaknesses.

JavaScript: The de facto language of the web offers widespread support and a vast ecosystem of libraries and frameworks. However, it can suffer from performance issues and lacks the strict type safety that Rust provides.

Python: Known for its simplicity and readability, Python excels in rapid development and has a rich array of web frameworks (like Flask and Django). However, it typically trades performance for ease of use, which may not be suitable for high-demand scenarios.

Ruby: With Rails, Ruby is celebrated for its developer-friendly conventions and productivity. However, Ruby is also subject to performance limitations when compared to Rust.

Rust provides an alternative for scenarios where performance and safety are paramount. While it may have a steeper learning curve compared to some of the more established web development languages, the benefits it offers in terms of performance and reliability can make it a compelling choice, particularly for backend development or performance-critical applications.

1.5 Getting Started with Rust

Getting started with Rust for web development involves the following steps:

Installation: Install Rust using `rustup`, the recommended toolchain installer. This provides a seamless way to manage Rust versions and associated components.

Setting up a New Project: Use `cargo`, Rust's package manager, to create and manage projects. Cargo simplifies building, testing, and managing dependencies.

Exploring Frameworks: Familiarize yourself with Rust's web frameworks. Start with basic applications to understand the paradigms and patterns these frameworks promote.

Hands-On Practice: Build simple applications or APIs to deepen your understanding of Rust's syntax, ownership model, and how to handle async operations.

Community and Resources: Utilize resources such as the Rust Book, documentation, forums, and community contributions to enhance your learning journey.

As web development continues to evolve, Rust presents exciting opportunities for developers seeking to leverage its performance and safety features. While there may be an initial learning curve, the advantages it offers for high-performing, secure web applications make it worth exploring.

Understanding Rust's Unique Features for Web Programming

While languages like JavaScript and Python have dominated the web development landscape, Rust's unique features present compelling advantages for building web applications that require performance, safety, and concurrency. In this chapter, we will delve into the distinctive characteristics of Rust that make it an ideal candidate for web programming, examining its memory safety, concurrency model, and ecosystem of libraries and tools that enhance web development.

Memory Safety Without a Garbage Collector

One of Rust's standout features is its approach to memory safety. Traditional memory management techniques, especially those reliant on garbage collectors, can lead to latency and performance overhead. Rust eliminates the need for garbage collection by using a sophisticated ownership model. This model ensures:

Safe Memory Management: Rust enforces strict rules about ownership, borrowing, and lifetimes, which minimize the risk of memory leaks and data races. Each piece of data has a single owner, and when ownership is transferred, Rust's compiler enforces these rules at compile time.

Zero-Cost Abstractions: The memory management in Rust introduces no runtime overhead, meaning that developers can achieve high levels of performance similar to C and C++ while retaining safety. This is especially beneficial in web programming where performance can critically impact user experience.

The memory safety guarantees of Rust make it particularly suitable for building back-end services where security and performance are paramount.

Concurrency with Confidence

Concurrency presents a significant challenge in web programming, where multiple tasks often need to be executed simultaneously without stepping on each other's toes. Rust's concurrency model is built around ownership and borrowing, ensuring that data is accessed in a safe manner.

Fearless Concurrency: Rust's type system prevents data races at compile time, enabling developers to write concurrent code confidently. Threads in Rust can operate on shared data without the usual pitfalls that come with shared-state concurrency, such as race conditions and deadlocks.

Asynchronous Programming: With the introduction of `async` and `await` syntax, Rust supports asynchronous programming paradigms effectively. This is particularly useful for web servers and applications handling numerous client requests efficiently. Libraries like `tokio` and `async-std` allow developers to build high-performance asynchronous applications that are scalable and responsive.

WebAssembly: Expanding Rust's Reach

Rust's ability to compile to WebAssembly (Wasm) is a

game-changer for web programming, allowing developers to write performance-critical components in Rust that can run in the browser. WebAssembly is a robust, portable compilation target designed to execute at near-native speeds.

Performance Benefits: WebAssembly enables developers to run computationally intensive tasks without incurring the performance penalties of JavaScript. Features such as SIMD (Single Instruction,

Multiple Data) can be utilized to maximize performance for numerical computations.

Interoperability with JavaScript: Fast interaction between Rust (compiled to Wasm) and JavaScript allows developers to leverage existing JavaScript libraries while still gaining the performance benefits of Rust. This means that developers can write WebAssembly modules for performance-critical functionalities while maintaining the flexibility of using JavaScript for other parts of their applications.

A Thriving Ecosystem

Rust boasts a rapidly growing ecosystem of libraries and frameworks that facilitate web development. Prominent in this arena is the web framework **Rocket**, which provides a type-safe, easy-to-use interface for building web applications. Another important library is **Actix**, known for its speed and scalability, allowing developers to create robust, asynchronous web servers.

Cargo: Rust's package manager, Cargo, simplifies dependency management and builds processes for web applications. With an easy command-line interface and a rich repository of libraries known as crates, developers can quickly scaffold their projects and integrate functionality with minimal setup.

Rich Tooling: The Rust tooling ecosystem, which includes `rustfmt` for code formatting and `clippy` for linting, enhances developer productivity. Coupled with an excellent compiler that provides detailed error messages and suggestions, the development workflow becomes smoother, leading to better-written web applications.

Community and Support

The safety, concurrency, compilation to WebAssembly, and a thriving ecosystem might be enticing, but the community that supports Rust plays an equally crucial role in its appeal for web programming. Rust's community is known for its inclusivity and willingness to help newcomers.

Documentation and Learning Resources: The official Rust documentation is comprehensive and continuously updated. The Rust Book is a widely recommended resource for new developers. Additionally, specialized online courses aimed at web programming with Rust are becoming more commonplace.

Active Forums and Discussion Channels: Active discussions on forums, including Reddit, Discord, and the Rust Users Forum, provide platforms for developers to share knowledge, troubleshoot issues, and foster collaborative projects.

Rust's unique features position it as a formidable player in the realm of web programming. Its commitment to memory safety, ability to handle concurrency efficiently, potential for WebAssembly integration, thriving ecosystem, and supportive community make it an attractive option for developers looking to build high-performance web applications.

Setting Up Your Rust Development Environment

Whether you are a seasoned developer looking to explore Rust or a newcomer interested in getting started, setting up your Rust development environment is the first crucial step. In this chapter, we will guide you through the process of installing and configuring the necessary tools, so you can begin writing Rust code effectively.

1. Prerequisites

Before diving into the setup, ensure that your system meets the following prerequisites:

Operating System: Rust is cross-platform and supports Windows, macOS, and Linux. Ensure your system is up to date.

Basic Command Line Knowledge: Familiarity with the command line will be beneficial as we will use it extensively.

Administrator Permissions: You may need administrative rights to install software on your system.
2. Installing Rust

The official way to install Rust is through `rustup`, a tool that manages Rust versions and associated tools. Follow these steps for installation:

Windows

Open PowerShell or Command Prompt as an administrator.

Download and run the `rustup` installer by executing:

```sh
curl --proto '=https' --tlsv1.2 -sSf https://sh.rustup.rs | sh
```

Follow the on-screen instructions. The default installation will be sufficient for most users. ### macOS

Open your terminal.

To install `rustup`, run:

```sh
curl --proto '=https' --tlsv1.2 -sSf https://sh.rustup.rs | sh
```

Accept the defaults in the installation wizard. ### Linux

Open your terminal.

Use curl to install `rustup`:

```sh
curl --proto '=https' --tlsv1.2 -sSf https://sh.rustup.rs | sh
```

Follow the prompt to complete the installation. ## 3. Configuring Your Environment

After installation, you'll need to configure your environment:

Update Your Path

The installation script will add the necessary configuration to your shell profile, but you may need to restart your terminal or execute:

- For `bash` or `zsh`:

```sh
source $HOME/.cargo/env
```

- For `fish`:

```sh
set -Ux PATH $PATH $HOME/.cargo/bin
```

Verify the Installation

To verify that Rust has been installed correctly, run the following command:

```sh
rustc --version
```

This should output the version of `rustc`, the Rust compiler, which confirms that your installation was successful.

4. Setting Up an Integrated Development Environment (IDE)

While you can code Rust using any text editor, using an IDE or advanced text editor enhances productivity with features like code completion, errors checking, and debugging. Here are popular options:

Visual Studio Code

Install Visual Studio Code from code.visualstudio.com.

Open VS Code and navigate to the Extensions panel (Ctrl+Shift+X).

Search for and install the "Rust (rls)" extension, which provides support for Rust development. ### IntelliJ IDEA

Download IntelliJ IDEA from [jetbrains.com](https://www.jetbrains.com/idea/).

Install the Rust plugin via `Preferences -> Plugins -> Marketplace` and search for "Rust". ### Other Editors

Atom has a Rust Language support plugin.

Sublime Text can be configured with Rust syntax highlighting and LSP support using a package manager.

5. Setting Up Your First Project

With Rust installed and your IDE configured, it's time to create your first Rust project. Rust uses Cargo, a package manager and build system, which is installed along with Rust.

Open your terminal.

Create a new Rust project with Cargo by running:

```sh
cargo new hello_rust
```

Navigate into your project directory:

```sh
cd hello_rust
```

Open the project in your chosen IDE. ## 6. Building and Running Your Project

You can build and run your Rust project using Cargo commands:

- To build the project, execute:

```sh
cargo build
```

- To run the project, use:

```sh cargo run
```

Your terminal should display "Hello, world!" if everything is set up correctly, as Cargo has generated the initial code for you.

7. Updating Rust

Rust is continually evolving, and keeping it updated is essential for accessing the latest features and fixes. You can update your Rust installation using the following command:

```sh
rustup update
```

Chapter 2: Getting Started with Web Frameworks in Rust

This chapter will serve as your guide to understanding the basic concepts of web frameworks in Rust, introducing you to their structure, features, and how to get started building your first web application.

2.1 Overview of Rust Web Frameworks

Before diving into specific frameworks, let's take a moment to explore what a web framework does. A web framework provides tools, libraries, and patterns that simplify the development of web applications. It typically includes functionalities for handling HTTP requests/responses, routing, templating, and middleware support.

In the Rust ecosystem, some popular web frameworks include:

Rocket: A web framework that emphasizes ergonomics, type safety, and developer productivity. Rocket is known for its ease of use and clean syntax.

Actix Web: A powerful, actor-based framework that provides high performance and is built on top of the Actix actor framework. It's suitable for applications requiring concurrent processing.

Warp: A minimalist, composable framework with a focus on type safety and async. It utilizes the Tokio async runtime.

Tide: An async web framework designed with

simplicity and ease of use in mind. It caters to those who prefer a straightforward approach to web development.

Nickel: A lightweight framework modeled after Express.js in Node.js. It's a great choice for smaller projects or when you need minimal overhead.

2.2 Setting Up Your Rust Environment

Before you can create a web application, you need to ensure that your development environment is ready. Here's a step-by-step guide to setting up Rust and a web framework.

2.2.1 Install Rust

If you haven't already, you'll need to install Rust. The recommended way is to use `rustup`, which manages Rust versions for you:

```bash
curl --proto '=https' --tlsv1.2 -sSf https://sh.rustup.rs | sh
```

After installation, set up your path by ensuring `~/.cargo/bin` is in your shell's PATH. ### 2.2.2 Creating a New Project

Once Rust is installed, you can create a new Rust project using Cargo, Rust's package manager and build system. Open your terminal and run:

```bash
cargo new rust_web_app cd rust_web_app
```

This will create a new directory with the basic structure of a Rust application. ### 2.2.3 Adding Dependencies

Depending on which framework you'd like to use, you will need to add it as a dependency in your

`Cargo.toml` file. For instance, if you decide to use Rocket, you would modify your `Cargo.toml` as follows:

```toml
[dependencies] rocket = "0.5.0"
```

For Actix Web:

```toml
[dependencies] actix-web = "4.0"
```

You'll want to check the respective documentation for the latest versions and additional dependencies you might need.

2.3 Building Your First Web Application

Let's build a simple web application using Rocket. This example will illustrate basic routing and returning a simple response.

2.3.1 Creating a Basic Rocket Application

Open the `src/main.rs` file and replace its content with the following:

```rust
#[macro_use] extern crate rocket;
```

```
#[get("/")]
fn index() -> &'static str { "Hello, world!"
}
#[launch]
fn rocket() -> _ {
rocket::build().mount("/", routes![index])
}
```

This code defines a single route `/` that returns a text response "Hello, world!" when accessed. ### 2.3.2 Running Your Application

To run your application, use the following command in your terminal:

```bash cargo run
```

This will compile your application and start a local web server. By default, Rocket runs on `http://localhost:8000`.

2.3.3 Accessing Your Application

Open your web browser and navigate to `http://localhost:8000`. You should see "Hello, world!" displayed on the webpage. Congratulations! You've successfully built your first web application in Rust using the Rocket framework.

2.4 Further Exploration

As you become more comfortable with basic routing, you

can explore more advanced features such as:

Database Integration: Most web applications require data storage. Rust provides several libraries for working with databases, such as Diesel and SQLx, which can be integrated into your web application.

Error Handling: Understanding how to handle errors gracefully in your application will improve user experience and maintainability.

Middleware: Add middleware for functions such as logging requests, handling CORS, or authentication.

Templates: Render dynamic HTML using template engines like Askama or Tera.

In this chapter, you started your journey into web development with Rust, setting up your environment and building a simple web application using the Rocket framework. The Rust ecosystem has a variety of frameworks and libraries that can help you build robust and efficient web applications.

As you progress, don't hesitate to dive deeper into the documentation of the framework you choose to understand advanced concepts and best practices. The Rust community is strong and continuously growing, providing ample resources and support as you develop your skills.

Introduction to Actix and Rocket Frameworks

Developed by Mozilla Research and first released in 2010, Rust has established itself as a go-to language for building reliable and high-performance applications. Its unique ownership model ensures memory safety without the need for a garbage collector, which is one of the reasons it is favored for systems-level programming.

As web applications proliferate, the demand for robust web frameworks that leverage the unique features of Rust has risen significantly. In this chapter, we will introduce two of the most popular web frameworks in the Rust ecosystem: Actix and Rocket. Both frameworks are designed to facilitate the development of web services and applications while providing distinct features and philosophies.

Actix Framework ### Overview

Actix is a powerful, pragmatic, and extremely fast actor-based framework for building concurrent and resilient applications. It is built on the Actix actor system, which allows developers to design applications as a network of independent actors that communicate through messages. This model makes Actix particularly suitable for applications that require high concurrency, such as real-time web applications and APIs.

Key Features

Actor Model: Actix uses the actor model, which simplifies the design of concurrent applications by encapsulating state and behavior within independent entities. This makes it easier to reason about state management and promotes isolation.

High Performance: Actix has been benchmarked as one of the fastest web frameworks available. Its performance is due in part to its minimal abstractions and extensive use of Rust's powerful type system.

Extensible: Actix is highly extensible, allowing developers to create middleware and integrate third-party libraries easily.

WebSocket Support: Actix has built-in support for WebSockets, making it excellent for developing real-time applications where bidirectional communication between the client and server is needed.

Use Cases

Actix is ideal for applications requiring scalability and resilience, such as gaming servers, microservices, and real-time notification systems. It is a suitable choice for developers looking to build high-performance APIs that can handle a significant amount of traffic.

Rocket Framework ### Overview

Rocket is another excellent web framework for Rust that emphasizes usability and developer productivity. Its design philosophy revolves around providing a clean and intuitive API while ensuring safety and performance. Rocket has established a reputation for its powerful routing and form handling capabilities, making it suitable for developing robust server-side applications.

Key Features

Type Safety: Rocket leverages Rust's strong type system to catch many errors at compile time. This feature significantly reduces runtime errors and enhances the reliability of the application.

Intuitive API: Rocket is designed to be user-friendly, with an expressive and declarative API that allows developers to define routes and handlers with minimal boilerplate.

Dynamic Routing: Rocket provides a powerful routing system that allows developers to define dynamic routes effortlessly. This feature is ideal for building RESTful APIs.

Customizable Middleware: Similar to Actix, Rocket allows for easy creation and integration of middleware. This capability provides flexibility in extending the framework's functionality.

Use Cases

Rocket is particularly well-suited for web applications that require rapid development cycles, such as content management systems, RESTful APIs, and web-based dashboards. Its emphasis on type safety and usability makes it attractive for developers who prioritize maintainability and ease of use.

Both Actix and Rocket represent the cutting edge of web development in Rust, each catering to different needs and preferences. Actix excels in scenarios demanding concurrency and performance, leveraging the actor model for effective state management. On the other hand, Rocket shines with its developer-friendly API and focus on safety, making it an attractive option for those looking to quickly build feature-rich applications.

Choosing the Right Framework for Your Project

Rust, known for its emphasis on safety, concurrency, and

high-performance systems, has several frameworks catering to different application domains, including web development, embedded systems, and command- line tools. This chapter aims to guide you through the considerations and factors that play a crucial role in selecting the right framework for your Rust project.

Understanding Your Project Requirements

Before diving into the specifics of the frameworks themselves, it is essential to outline the basic requirements of your project. Consider the following questions:

What type of application are you building?

Is it a web application, CLI tool, library, embedded software, or something else entirely?

What are the performance needs?

Does your application require real-time capabilities? How critical is throughput and latency?

What is your team's skill level?

Is your team proficient in Rust, or is everyone new to the language? Some frameworks have a steeper learning curve than others.

What are your long-term maintenance goals?

Consider how easy the framework is to maintain, document, and extend over time.

Are there any specific integrations you need?

Does your project need to interface with existing systems, databases, or external services? ## Evaluating Popular Rust Frameworks

1. **Web Frameworks**

For web development, Rust offers several frameworks that cater to different needs:

Rocket: Known for its ease of use and developer-friendly features, Rocket allows for fast prototyping and building secure web applications. Its syntax is quite expressive, and it provides great tooling, but note that it requires the use of the nightly version of Rust.

Actix Web: This framework is well-suited for high-performance applications. It's built on the Actix actor framework, allowing for efficient handling of concurrent connections. While it can have a steeper learning curve due to its complexity, its performance is unmatched.

Warp: A lightweight and composable web framework, Warp is ideal for microservices and offers a flexible way to handle HTTP requests. It uses a functional programming style, which may appeal to certain developers but can also intimidate others.

2. **CLI Tool Frameworks**

If you're developing command-line applications, consider:

Clap: The most widely used library for parsing command-line arguments in Rust. Its builder pattern is intuitive and helps you create robust command-line interfaces.

StructOpt: Built on top of Clap, this library utilizes Rust's derive macros to simplify argument parsing. It's ideal for those who prefer a more declarative style.

3. **Data Handling and Serialization**

For projects involving data handling and serialization, look into:

Serde: This framework is a cornerstone for serialization in Rust. It allows you to convert complex data structures into formats like JSON, YAML, and more. Given Rust's strong typing, Serde handles data efficiently and safely, making it essential for data-driven applications.

4. **Embedded Systems Frameworks**

If your focus is on embedded systems, consider:

Embedded Rust: A collection of resources, libraries, and frameworks designed specifically for embedded systems. The `no_std` paradigm (which excludes the standard library) allows for lightweight applications in constrained environments.

Rust's embedded ecosystem: The `embedded-hal` crate provides traits for common hardware abstractions, making it easier to write portable and safe embedded code.

Performance Considerations

Performance is often a deciding factor in choosing a framework. While Rust inherently provides great performance potential due to its zero-cost abstractions and efficient memory management, different frameworks might affect runtime characteristics. Always benchmark frameworks under realistic conditions relevant to your specific use case before making a choice.

Community and Ecosystem

The community around a framework can provide valuable resources, libraries, and support. Consider:

Documentation Quality: Comprehensive and clear documentation can significantly reduce onboarding time for new developers.

Community Activity: A vibrant community means more plugins, third-party libraries, and an ecosystem that evolves with input from its users.

Long-term Viability

Technology is ever-evolving, and frameworks can become obsolete or fall out of favor. Check the framework's activity on platforms such as GitHub or crates.io, looking for regular updates, bug fixes, and the frequency of new releases. Stability and long-term support are crucial for projects that will be in production for years.

By thoroughly evaluating the options available and aligning them with your project requirements, you can ensure that your chosen framework contributes positively to the success and sustainability of your project. This decision is a pivotal step towards building robust, efficient, and maintainable applications in Rust.

Chapter 3: Building Your First Web Server

In this chapter, we will venture into the exciting world of web development using Rust. Rust has gained popularity in the realm of system programming and web development due to its emphasis on performance and memory safety. By the end of this chapter, you will have a solid understanding of how to build a simple web server in Rust, as well as a clearer perspective on the underlying concepts that make it work.

3.1 Introduction to Rust Web Development

Before diving into the code, it's essential to understand why Rust is an excellent choice for web development. Rust offers several advantages, including:

Memory Safety: Rust's ownership model prevents common programming errors, such as null pointer dereferences and buffer overflows.

Concurrency: Rust's threading model allows safe concurrent programming, which is critical for scalable web servers.

Performance: Compared to many other programming languages, Rust can offer performance close to C/C++ due to its ability to compile to native code.

These features make Rust particularly well-suited for building web servers that require high performance and reliability.

3.2 Setting Up Your Rust Environment

To get started, make sure you have Rust installed on your

machine. You can install Rust using `rustup`, which is a tool for managing Rust versions and associated tools. Follow these steps:

Open your terminal.

Run the following command:

```sh
curl --proto '=https' --tlsv1.2 -sSf https://sh.rustup.rs | sh
```

After installation, ensure that your PATH is set up correctly:

```sh
source $HOME/.cargo/env
```

Check your installation by running:

```sh
rustc --version
```

Once you have confirmed that Rust is installed, we can create our web server project. ## 3.3 Creating a New Rust Project

To create a new Rust project, we'll use Cargo, Rust's package manager and build system. Follow these steps:

Run the following command in your terminal:

```sh
cargo new rust_web_server
```

This command creates a new directory called `rust_web_server` with a basic Rust project structure.

Navigate into the project directory:

```sh
cd rust_web_server
```

Open the project in your favorite code editor. ## 3.4 Adding Dependencies

To build a web server, we'll use a popular Rust web framework called **Actix-web**. This framework is powerful, efficient, and widely used in the Rust community. Modify your `Cargo.toml` file to include the Actix-web dependency:

```toml [dependencies] actix-web = "4"
```

This tells Cargo to download the Actix-web library when you build your project. ## 3.5 Building the Web Server

With our dependencies set up, we are ready to begin coding. Open `src/main.rs` and replace its contents with the following code:

```rust
use actix_web::{web, App, HttpServer, HttpResponse};
```

```rust
async fn greet() -> HttpResponse {

HttpResponse::Ok().body("Hello, welcome to your first
Rust web server!")

}

#[actix_web::main]

async    fn    main()    ->    std::io::Result<()>    {
HttpServer::new(|| {

App::new().route("/", web::get().to(greet))

})

.bind("127.0.0.1:8080")?

.run()

.await

}
```
` ` `

Understanding the Code

Imports: The code begins by importing necessary
components from the Actix-web library.

Async Function: The `greet` function is defined as an
asynchronous handler for incoming requests. It responds
with a simple text message.

Main Function: In the `main` function:

We create a new HTTP server that listens on
`127.0.0.1:8080`.

We define a routing mechanism that maps the root URL
`/` to our `greet` function.

Finally, we run the server.

3.6 Running Your Web Server

Now that you've written your first web server in Rust, it's time to run it!

In your terminal, execute the following command:

```sh
cargo run
```

You should see output indicating that the server is running. Open your web browser and navigate to

`http://127.0.0.1:8080/`. You should see a message: "Hello, welcome to your first Rust web server!" ## 3.7 Testing the Web Server

To test the web server further, you can use tools like `curl` or Postman. For example, you can run the following command in another terminal:

```sh
curl http://127.0.0.1:8080/
```

You should receive the same greeting message printed in your terminal.

Congratulations! You have successfully built and run your first web server in Rust. In this chapter, we covered key steps, including setting up your environment, creating a new project, adding dependencies, building the server, and testing it. This foundational understanding prepares you for more complex web applications in Rust.

As you advance further into Rust web development,

consider exploring more features of Actix-web, such as handling different HTTP methods, routing, middleware, and connecting with databases. Rust's robustness will enable you to create effective and efficient web applications that can stand the test of time.

Setting Up a Basic HTTP Server Using Actix

Rust, known for its performance and safety, provides several frameworks for web development, with Actix being one of the most popular choices. In this chapter, we'll walk through the steps to set up a basic HTTP server using Actix in Rust. We will cover everything from initial setup to handling routing and responding to HTTP requests.

1. Why Choose Actix?

Actix is a powerful actor-based framework for Rust that offers high performance due to its async capabilities and efficient resource utilization. Its features include:

Speed: Actix is one of the fastest web frameworks available, making it suitable for high-performance applications.

Flexibility: It allows developers to choose how they want to handle things like routing, middleware, and error handling.

Ecosystem: Actix provides a rich set of libraries for building complex applications while ensuring type safety.

2. Setting Up Your Environment

Before we begin, ensure that you have the latest version of Rust installed. You can do this by using `rustup`, Rust's official toolchain installer.

Install Rust:

If you haven't installed Rust yet, follow the instructions available on the official [Rust installation page](https://www.rust-lang.org/tools/install).

Create a New Rust Project:

Open your terminal and run the following command to create a new project:

```bash
cargo new actix_http_server cd actix_http_server
```

3. Adding Actix Dependencies

The next step is to configure your project by adding Actix dependencies. Open `Cargo.toml` in your project directory and add the following lines under `[dependencies]`:

```toml
[dependencies] actix-web = "4.0"
tokio = { version = "1", features = ["full"] }
```

This code tells Cargo to download and compile Actix web framework and Tokio, which is an asynchronous runtime needed to run the Actix server.

4. Creating a Basic HTTP Server

Now that you have your dependencies set up, you can create a basic HTTP server. Create a new file

`src/main.rs` and replace its content with the following code:

```rust
use actix_web::{web, App, HttpServer, HttpResponse};
#[actix_web::main]
async fn main() -> std::io::Result<()> {
HttpServer::new(|| {
App::new()
.route("/", web::get().to(greet))
})
.bind("127.0.0.1:8080")?
.run()
.await
}
async fn greet() -> HttpResponse {
HttpResponse::Ok().body("Hello, Actix!")
}
```

Explanation of the Code:

Imports: The necessary types from `actix_web` are imported.

Main Function: An `async` main function is defined using `#[actix_web::main]` which sets up the Actix runtime.

HttpServer: The `HttpServer` binds to the address `127.0.0.1:8080` and initializes an application using a closure.

41

Route Handling: A route is defined with `web::get().to(greet)`, which means that an HTTP GET request to the root path (`/`) will trigger the `greet` function.

Greet Function: This function returns an HTTP response with the body "Hello, Actix!". ## 5. Running the Server

You can now run your server. In the terminal, from your project directory, execute:

```bash
cargo run
```

You should see output indicating that the server is running on `127.0.0.1:8080`. Open a web browser or use a tool like `curl` to access `http://127.0.0.1:8080`. You should see the message "Hello, Actix!".

6. Adding More Routes

To demonstrate how to add more functionality, let's enhance our server by adding routes. Update the `main.rs` file like this:

```rust
use actix_web::{web, App, HttpServer, HttpResponse};

#[actix_web::main]
async fn main() -> std::io::Result<()> {
```

```rust
HttpServer::new(|| { App::new()
.route("/", web::get().to(greet))
.route("/farewell", web::get().to(farewell))
})
.bind("127.0.0.1:8080")?
.run()
.await
}

async fn greet() -> HttpResponse {
HttpResponse::Ok().body("Hello, Actix!")
}

async fn farewell() -> HttpResponse {
HttpResponse::Ok().body("Goodbye, Actix!")
}
```

Now, when you navigate to `http://127.0.0.1:8080/farewell`, you should see "Goodbye, Actix!". ## 7. Handling Parameters

Actix allows you to handle URL parameters easily. Let's add a route that takes a name as a path parameter:

```rust
async fn greet_name(web::Path(name): web::Path<String>) -> HttpResponse {
HttpResponse::Ok().body(format!("Hello, {}!", name))
}
```

```
HttpServer::new(|| { App::new()
.route("/", web::get().to(greet))
.route("/farewell", web::get().to(farewell))
.route("/greet/{name}", web::get().to(greet_name))
})
```
```

With this change, visiting
`http://127.0.0.1:8080/greet/{your_name}` will
personalize the greeting.

In this chapter, we successfully set up a basic HTTP server using the Actix framework in Rust. We covered:

How to create a new Rust project and add Actix dependencies.

The fundamentals of creating routes and handling requests.

Adding dynamic routing to personalize responses.

With a firm understanding of these basics, you can now further explore Actix's rich features, such as middleware, error handling, and database integration, to create more complex web applications. Actix provides the scalability and performance needed for modern web development, making it a great choice as you advance in your Rust programming journey.

## Building a Simple Web Application with Rocket
```

One of the compelling features of Rust is its rich ecosystem that includes frameworks for web development. One such framework is Rocket, which emphasizes ease of use and a strong type system. In this chapter, we will build a simple web application using Rocket, guiding you through the installation process, creating basic routes, handling requests, and deploying your application.

Setting up Your Environment

Before we dive into the code, we need to ensure that our development environment is set up correctly. ### Installing Rust

If you haven't already installed Rust, you can do so using `rustup`, Rust's official installer and version management tool. Follow these steps:

Open your terminal.

Run the following command to download and install Rust:

```bash
curl --proto '=https' --tlsv1.2 -sSf https://sh.rustup.rs | sh
```

Follow the on-screen instructions to complete the installation.

After installation, ensure that your PATH is set up correctly by running:

```bash
source $HOME/.cargo/env
```

You can check your installation with:

```bash
rustc --version
```

Creating a New Project

Once Rust is installed, we can create a new Rocket project. Open your terminal and run the following commands:

```bash
cargo new simple_rocket_app cd simple_rocket_app
```

This command creates a new directory called `simple_rocket_app` with a basic Rust project structure. ### Adding Rocket to Your Project

Rocket will not be part of the standard Rust library, so we need to add it as a dependency. Open `Cargo.toml` in your project's root directory and add the following lines:

```toml
[dependencies]
rocket = "0.5.0-rc.1" # Check for the latest version on crates.io
```

Now that we have Rocket included in our project, let's create our first web application. ## Building the Web Application

Creating a Basic Rocket Application

In the `src/main.rs` file, we will write our basic Rocket web application. Here is what our complete file might look

like:

```rust
#[macro_use] extern crate rocket;
#[get("/")]
fn index() -> &'static str {
"Hello, world! Welcome to my Rocket application."
}
#[launch]
fn rocket() -> _ { rocket::build().mount("/",
routes![index])
}
```

Explanation of the Code

#[macro_use] extern crate rocket;: This line imports Rocket's macros, which allows us to use the

`#[get]` and `#[launch]` attributes.

#[get("/")]: This attribute defines an HTTP GET route at the root URL (`/`).

fn index() -> &'static str: This function handles requests to the root route, returning a static string.

#[launch] fn rocket() -> _: This attribute marks our main function for starting the Rocket application. The function builds the Rocket instance and mounts our routes.

Running the Application

To run your Rocket application, return to your terminal and execute:

47

```bash cargo run
```

You should see output indicating that Rocket is up and running. By default, it will be accessible at `http://localhost:8000`.

Testing the Application

Open a web browser or use a tool like `curl` to access the root route:

```bash
curl http://localhost:8000
```

You should see the message:
```

Hello, world! Welcome to my Rocket application.
```

Adding More Functionality

Now that we have the basic application up and running, let's add some more functionality by creating another route and handling query parameters.

Adding a Greeting Route

We can extend our application by adding a greeting route. Modify your `main.rs` like this:

```rust #[get("/greet?<name>")]

fn greet(name: Option<String>) -> String { match name {
```

```
Some(n) => format!("Hello, {}!", n), None => "Hello,
stranger!".to_string(),
    }
}
#[launch]
fn rocket() -> _ {
rocket::build().mount("/", routes![index, greet])
}
```

Explanation of the New Code

#[get("/greet?<name>")]: This route captures a query
parameter named `name`.

fn greet(name: Option<String>) -> String: The
`greet` function checks if the `name` parameter is
present and responds accordingly.

After saving your changes, restart your application with
`cargo run`. ### Testing the Greeting Route

You can test the new greeting functionality by accessing
the route with a query parameter:

```bash
curl "http://localhost:8000/greet?name=John"
```

This should return:
```

Hello, John!
```

```
```
If you access the route without a name, like this:
```bash
curl "http://localhost:8000/greet"
```

You will see:
```
Hello, stranger!
```

In this chapter, we built a simple web application using Rocket in Rust. We set up our development environment, created basic routes, and even handled query parameters. Rocket's straightforward and intuitive syntax makes it a powerful choice for web development in Rust. As you continue to explore Rocket, consider extending your application further by implementing more complex features, such as handling form submissions or connecting to a database.

Chapter 4: REST API Development Fundamentals

Representational State Transfer (REST) is a widely adopted architectural style for designing networked applications. This chapter explores the fundamentals of developing RESTful APIs using Rust, a systems programming language known for its performance, safety, and concurrency features.

In this chapter, we will cover the key concepts of REST APIs, the advantages of using Rust for API development, and provide a step-by-step guide on setting up a simple RESTful service. Additionally, we will look at common practices, tools, and libraries that can streamline the development process.

Understanding REST Principles

Before diving into the code, it is crucial to understand the core principles of REST APIs:

Statelessness: Each API request from the client must contain all the information the server needs to fulfill that request. The server does not store the client's state.

Resource-Based: In REST, every piece of data is treated as a resource, which is identifiable via a unique URI (Uniform Resource Identifier).

HTTP Methods: REST APIs leverage standard HTTP methods:

`GET` for fetching data

`POST` for creating new resources

`PUT` for updating existing resources

`DELETE` for removing resources

Representations: While resources themselves are abstract concepts, they can be represented in various formats (e.g., JSON, XML). JSON is the most common format for web APIs today.

Hypermedia as the Engine of Application State (HATEOAS): Clients interact with the API dynamically through hyperlinks that guide them to available operations.

Advantages of Using Rust for REST API Development

Rust offers several benefits that make it an attractive choice for building RESTful services:

Performance: Rust's zero-cost abstractions and direct compilation to machine code result in high performance, rivaling C and C++.

Memory Safety: With its ownership model, Rust helps prevent common programming errors, such as null pointer dereferencing and data races, leading to more secure applications.

Concurrency: Rust provides powerful concurrency primitives, making it easier to write multi-threaded applications without the risk of runtime data races.

Tooling and Ecosystem: The Rust ecosystem is rich with libraries (crates) like `Actix-Web`, `Rocket`, and `Warp` that facilitate quick and efficient API development.

Setting Upa Simple RESTful API in Rust ### Prerequisites

Ensure you have Rust installed on your system. You can follow the instructions at https://www.rust-lang.org/tools/install. For this chapter, we will use the `Actix-Web` framework, which is simple yet powerful.

Step 1: Create a New Rust Project

Open your terminal and create a new Rust project:

```bash
cargo new rust_api cd rust_api
```

Step 2: Update the `Cargo.toml` File

Add the `Actix-Web` dependency to your `Cargo.toml` file:

```toml
[dependencies] actix-web = "4.0"
serde = { version = "1.0", features = ["derive"] }
serde_json = "1.0"
```

Step 3: Create a Basic API

In the `src/main.rs` file, replace its content with the following code:

```rust
use actix_web::{web, App, HttpServer, HttpResponse, Responder}; use serde::{Serialize, Deserialize};

#[derive(Serialize, Deserialize)] struct Item {
id: u32, name: String,
}
```

53

```rust
#[get("/item/{id}")]
async fn get_item(web::Path(id): web::Path<u32>) ->
impl Responder { let item = Item {

id,

name: String::from("Sample Item"),

};

HttpResponse::Ok().json(item) // Return item as JSON

}
#[post("/item")]
async fn create_item(item: web::Json<Item>) -> impl
Responder                                          {
HttpResponse::Created().json(item.into_inner()) // Echo
back the created item

}
#[actix_web::main]
async fn main() -> std::io::Result<()> {


HttpServer::new(|| { App::new()

.service(get_item)

.service(create_item)

})

.bind("127.0.0.1:8080")?

.run()

.await
```

```
}
```

Step 4: Run the API

In your terminal, run the following command:

```bash
cargo run
```

Your API should now be running at `http://127.0.0.1:8080`. You can test it using `curl` or a tool like Postman.

Step 5: Testing the API

To test your API, open another terminal or tool and:

GET request to fetch an item:

```bash
curl http://127.0.0.1:8080/item/1
```

POST request to create an item:

```bash
curl -X POST http://127.0.0.1:8080/item -H "Content-Type: application/json" -d '{"id":1,"name":"Test Item"}'
```

Best Practices

When developing REST APIs in Rust, consider the following best practices:

Error Handling: Use `Result` and `Option` types effectively for better error management.

Logging: Implement structured logging to help with monitoring and debugging.

Security: Ensure proper input validation, authentication, and authorization mechanisms.

Versioning: Plan for API versioning to manage breaking changes without affecting existing clients.

Testing: Write unit and integration tests to verify your API's functionality and performance.

In this chapter, we covered the fundamentals of REST API development in Rust, including key principles, advantages of Rust, and a practical example of building a simple service with Actix-Web. With its performance, safety features, and a growing ecosystem, Rust is well-suited for developing robust, scalable APIs. As you continue your journey in Rust programming, remember to adhere to best practices that will help you build APIs that stand the test of time.

Designing RESTful Endpoints with Actix

The focus will be on creating a simple REST API, understanding the principles behind REST, and leveraging Actix's features to create efficient and maintainable code.

Understanding REST Principles

Before diving into code, it's important to grasp the underlying principles of REST:

Statelessness: Each request from a client must contain all the information needed to process it. The server should not store client context between requests.

Resources and URIs: In RESTful architecture, everything is treated as a resource. Resources are identified by URIs (Uniform Resource Identifiers), and clients interact with them using standard HTTP methods: GET, POST, PUT, DELETE, etc.

Representation: Clients interact with resources through representations, usually in formats like JSON or XML. The server will send a representation of the resource on request, and clients can send representations to update resources.

HTTP Status Codes: Proper use of HTTP status codes provides clear communication about the outcome of API requests.

Setting Up the Actix Project

To begin, we need to set up a new Actix project. Make sure you have Rust and Cargo installed. To create a new project, run the following command:

```bash
cargo new actix_rest_api cd actix_rest_api
```

Next, we need to add Actix dependencies in `Cargo.toml`. Open this file and add:

```toml
[dependencies] actix-web = "4.0"
serde = { version = "1.0", features = ["derive"] }
```

```
serde_json = "1.0"
```

These dependencies include Actix for web server functionality and Serde for serialization and deserialization of JSON data.

Defining the Data Models

Let's create a simple API to manage a collection of books. We will define a `Book` struct to represent our data model. Create a new file `src/models.rs`:

```rust
use serde::{Serialize, Deserialize};

#[derive(Serialize, Deserialize, Clone)] pub struct Book {

pub id: usize, pub title: String,

pub author: String,

}
```

This model includes three fields: `id`, `title`, and `author`, all of which will be serialized to and from JSON.

Implementing the API

Next, we will implement the RESTful endpoints for creating, retrieving, updating, and deleting books. Let's create a new file `src/main.rs`:

```rust
use actix_web::{web, App, HttpServer, HttpResponse, Responder}; use std::sync::Mutex;
```

```rust
use std::collections::HashMap; use models::Book;

mod models; struct AppState {

books: Mutex<HashMap<usize, Book>>,

next_id: Mutex<usize>,

}

async fn get_books(data: web::Data<AppState>) -> impl
Responder { let books = data.books.lock().unwrap();

let books_list: Vec<Book> =
books.values().cloned().collect();
HttpResponse::Ok().json(books_list)

}

async fn get_book(path: web::Path<usize>, data:
web::Data<AppState>) -> impl Responder { let books =
data.books.lock().unwrap();

if let Some(book) = books.get(&path.into_inner()) {
HttpResponse::Ok().json(book)

} else {

HttpResponse::NotFound().finish()

}

}

async fn create_book(book: web::Json<Book>, data:
web::Data<AppState>) -> impl Responder { let mut books
= data.books.lock().unwrap();

let mut next_id = data.next_id.lock().unwrap();

let new_book = Book { id: *next_id,

title: book.title.clone(), author: book.author.clone(),
```

```rust
};
books.insert(*next_id, new_book.clone());
*next_id += 1; HttpResponse::Created().json(new_book)
}
async fn update_book( path: web::Path<usize>, book:
web::Json<Book>,
data: web::Data<AppState>,
) -> impl Responder {
let mut books = data.books.lock().unwrap(); let id =
path.into_inner();
if books.contains_key(&id) { let updated_book = Book {
id,
title: book.title.clone(), author: book.author.clone(),
};
books.insert(id,                    updated_book.clone());
HttpResponse::Ok().json(updated_book)
} else {
HttpResponse::NotFound().finish()
}
}
async fn delete_book(path: web::Path<usize>, data:
web::Data<AppState>) -> impl Responder { let mut books
= data.books.lock().unwrap();
if     books.remove(&path.into_inner()).is_some()     {
```

```rust
        HttpResponse::NoContent().finish()
    } else {
        HttpResponse::NotFound().finish()
    }
}
#[actix_web::main]
async fn main() -> std::io::Result<()> {
    let app_state = web::Data::new(AppState { books:
    Mutex::new(HashMap::new()), next_id: Mutex::new(0),
    });
    HttpServer::new(move || { App::new()
        .app_data(app_state.clone())
        .route("/books", web::get().to(get_books))
        .route("/books", web::post().to(create_book))
        .route("/books/{id}", web::get().to(get_book))
        .route("/books/{id}", web::put().to(update_book))
        .route("/books/{id}", web::delete().to(delete_book))
    })

    .bind("127.0.0.1:8080")?
    .run()
    .await
}
```

```
```

In this implementation, we define several handlers for our API endpoints:

** `get_books` **: Returns a list of all books.

** `get_book` **: Retrieves a book by its ID.

** `create_book` **: Adds a new book to the collection.

** `update_book` **: Updates an existing book by its ID.

** `delete_book` **: Deletes a book by its ID.

We use `Mutex` to ensure thread-safe access to shared state, allowing multiple requests to interact with the data concurrently.

Testing the API

After running the server with `cargo run`, you can test the API using tools like `curl` or Postman. Here are some example commands:

Create a Book

```bash
curl -X POST http://127.0.0.1:8080/books -H "Content-Type: application/json" -d '{"title": "The Rust Programming Language", "author": "Steve Klabnik and Carol Nichols"}'
```

Get All Books

```bash
curl -X GET http://127.0.0.1:8080/books
```

Get a Book by ID

```bash
curl -X GET http://127.0.0.1:8080/books/0
```

Update a Book

```bash
curl -X PUT http://127.0.0.1:8080/books/0 -H "Content-Type: application/json" -d '{"title": "The Rust Programming Language (Updated)", "author": "Steve Klabnik"}'
```

Delete a Book

```bash
curl -X DELETE http://127.0.0.1:8080/books/0
```

This serves as a foundation for further development and more complex back-end systems in Rust, demonstrating the language's capabilities for building reliable web services. With Actix, developers can leverage Rust's strong type system and concurrency model to create efficient, high-performance applications.

Implementing API Routes and Handlers with Rocket

In modern web development, APIs serve as the backbone for communication between different parts of an application—be it a frontend UI, a mobile app, or various microservices. Rust, with its focus on safety and performance, has emerged as a compelling choice for developing web applications. In this chapter, we will explore how to implement API routes and handlers using the Rocket web framework, which is known for its ease of use and full-featured support for creating web applications in Rust.

Setting Up the Rocket Project

Before diving into code, we need to set up our Rocket project. If you haven't already, ensure you have [Rust](https://www.rust-lang.org/tools/install) installed on your system. Then, create a new Rust project using Cargo, Rust's package manager:

```bash

cargo new rocket_api_example cd rocket_api_example
```

In your `Cargo.toml` file, you will need to add Rocket as a dependency. As of this writing, the latest stable version is `0.5`. Here's how your `Cargo.toml` should look:

```toml
[package]

name = "rocket_api_example" version = "0.1.0"

edition = "2021"

[dependencies]

rocket = "0.5.0-rc.1"  # Check for the latest version tokio = { version = "1", features = ["full"] }
```

Next, we need to include the features necessary for JSON support and configuring our Rocket application to run with the required runtime dependencies. Modify the `rocket` dependency to include the JSON feature:

```toml
[dependencies]
rocket = { version = "0.5.0-rc.1", features = ["json"] }
```

Creating Basic API Handlers

Now that we have set up our project, let's write some code. We will create a simple RESTful API with one resource: a `User`. This API will support GET, POST, and DELETE operations.

Structs and JSON Serialization

First, define a `User` struct along with the necessary HTTP handler functions; make sure to use Serde for JSON serialization.

Create a new file called `main.rs` inside the `src` directory:

```rust
#[macro_use] extern crate rocket;

use rocket::serde::{json::Json, Serialize, Deserialize}; use rocket::State;

use std::sync::Mutex;

use std::collections::HashMap;

#[derive(Debug, Serialize, Deserialize)] struct User {

id: u32, name: String,

}
```

```rust
// Define a type for our in-memory user store type
UserStore = Mutex<HashMap<u32, User>>;

#[post("/users", format = "json", data = "<user>")]
async fn create_user(user: Json<User>, state:
&State<UserStore>) -> String { let mut store =
state.lock().unwrap();

store.insert(user.id, user.into_inner());


format!("User {} created!", user.id)
}
#[get("/users/<id>")]
async fn get_user(id: u32, state: &State<UserStore>) ->
Option<Json<User>> { let store = state.lock().unwrap();

store.get(&id).cloned().map(Json)
}
#[delete("/users/<id>")]
async fn delete_user(id: u32, state: &State<UserStore>) -
> String { let mut store = state.lock().unwrap();

if store.remove(&id).is_some() { format!("User {}
deleted!", id)
} else {
format!("User {} not found!", id)
}
}
```
```
```

In this code snippet, we define the `User` struct, the API handlers, and a mutex-protected `UserStore` to hold our users in memory.

Mounting the API Routes

Now that we have the basic handlers ready, we need to mount these routes into our Rocket application. We'll also initialize the `UserStore` within the Rocket launch routine:

```rust
#[launch]

fn rocket() -> _ {

let user_store = UserStore::default();

rocket::build()

.manage(user_store)

.mount("/api", routes![create_user, get_user, delete_user])

}
```

Here, we're using the `manage` method to inject shared state (the `UserStore`) into our application. We then mount the routes at the `/api` endpoint.

Testing the API

To test the API, you can use tools like Postman, CURL, or HTTPie. Below are some sample commands:

Create a User:

```bash
curl -X POST http://localhost:8000/api/users -H
```

"Content-Type: application/json" -d '{"id": 1, "name": "John Doe"}'
```

**Get a User:**

```bash
curl -X GET http://localhost:8000/api/users/1
```

Delete a User:

```bash
curl -X DELETE http://localhost:8000/api/users/1
```

We set up a project, defined routes and handlers for user management, and provided mechanisms for testing our API endpoints. Rocket's intuitive design makes it a powerful tool for developing web applications in Rust, allowing developers to focus on building rather than configuration.
```

Chapter 5: Authentication and Authorization

Building robust authentication and authorization mechanisms is essential for protecting sensitive data and maintaining user trust. In this chapter, we will explore how to implement authentication and authorization in Rust web applications using popular libraries and best practices.

5.1 Understanding Authentication and Authorization

Before diving into implementation, it's important to differentiate between authentication and authorization:

Authentication is the process of verifying the identity of a user or system. It typically involves prompting the user for credentials, such as a username and password, and confirming that they are valid.

Authorization occurs after authentication and determines what an authenticated user is permitted to do. This typically involves checking their roles or permissions against the actions they are attempting to take.

5.2 Choosing the Right Framework

When developing web applications in Rust, the choice of web framework heavily influences how you handle authentication and authorization. Two popular frameworks are:

Actix Web: A powerful and flexible actor-based framework that is suitable for building asynchronous web applications.

Rocket: A productivity-oriented web framework that

focuses on ease of use and type safety, providing many features out-of-the-box.

For this chapter, we will provide examples using Actix Web, but similar concepts can be applied to Rocket and other frameworks.

5.3 Setting Up the Project

To get started, you'll need to create a new Rust project. Here's how to set up a basic Actix Web application:

```bash
cargo new rust_auth_example cd rust_auth_example
```

Then, add the required dependencies to your `Cargo.toml`:

```toml
[dependencies] actix-web = "4.0"
actix-session = "0.6"
bcrypt = "0.10"
serde = { version = "1.0", features = ["derive"] }
serde_json = "1.0"
```

5.4 Implementing User Registration

First, let's implement a simple user registration mechanism. In a real application, you would typically store user data in a database, but for simplicity, we will store users in memory.

5.4.1 Defining User Struct

Create a struct for user data with hashed passwords:

```rust
use bcrypt::{hash, verify, DEFAULT_COST};
#[derive(Debug, Serialize, Deserialize)] struct User {
username: String, password_hash: String,
}
```

5.4.2 Registration Handler

Next, create a handler for user registration. Here's how to implement a basic registration endpoint:

```rust
use actix_web::{post, web, App, HttpServer,
HttpResponse, Responder}; use std::sync::Mutex;
use std::collections::HashMap;
struct AppState {
users: Mutex<HashMap<String, User>>,
}
#[post("/register")]
async fn register(user: web::Json<User>, data:
web::Data<AppState>) -> impl Responder { let mut users
= data.users.lock().unwrap();

if users.contains_key(&user.username) {
return HttpResponse::Conflict().body("User already
exists");
}
```

```rust
let password_hash = hash(&user.password_hash,
DEFAULT_COST).unwrap(); let new_user = User {

username: user.username.clone(), password_hash,

};

users.insert(user.username.clone(),           new_user);
HttpResponse::Created().body("User           registered
successfully")

}
```
` ` `

5.5 Implementing Authentication

Once users can register, the next step is to implement authentication.

5.5.1 Authentication Handler

Create an endpoint that checks the credentials provided by the user:

` ` `rust #[post("/login")]

```rust
async fn login(user: web::Json<User>, data:
web::Data<AppState>) -> impl Responder { let users =
data.users.lock().unwrap();


if let Some(stored_user) = users.get(&user.username) {

if                      verify(&user.password_hash,
&stored_user.password_hash).unwrap()      {      return
HttpResponse::Ok().body("Login successful");

}

}
```

72

```
HttpResponse::Unauthorized().body("Invalid  username
or password")
}
```
```

## 5.6 Implementing Session Management

After a successful login, you'll typically want to maintain
the session for the authenticated user. Actix Web offers
middleware for session management.

### 5.6.1 Setting Up Sessions

You'll need to configure sessions and create a login
session for users after they log in:

```rust
use actix_session::{Session, SessionMiddleware}; use
actix_web::middleware::Logger;

#[actix_web::main]

async fn main() -> std::io::Result<()> { let data =
web::Data::new(AppState {

users: Mutex::new(HashMap::new()),

});

HttpServer::new(move || { App::new()

.app_data(data.clone())

.wrap(SessionMiddleware::new(
CookiesSessionStore::default(), Key::generate(),

))

.wrap(Logger::default())
```
```

```
.service(register)
.service(login)
})
.bind("127.0.0.1:8080")?
.run()
.await
}
```

5.7 Implementing Authorization

Now that we have authentication in place, let's implement authorization. This typically involves checking user roles before allowing access to certain endpoints.

5.7.1 Defining Roles

You can enhance the User struct to include roles:

```rust
#[derive(Debug, Serialize, Deserialize)] struct User {
username: String, password_hash: String,
role: String, // e.g., "admin", "user"
}
```

5.7.2 Authorize Middleware

You can create middleware to verify whether a user has the right role to access a particular route:

74

```rust
async fn auth_middleware(req: HttpRequest, session:
Session) -> Result<(), HttpResponse> { let username:
Option<String> = session.get("username").unwrap();

if username.is_none() {

return
Err(req.error_response(HttpResponse::Unauthorized()));

}
// Additional role checks can be implemented here Ok(())

}
```

In this chapter, we have covered how to implement authentication and authorization in a Rust web application using Actix Web. We looked at user registration, login handlers, session management, and role-based access control.

Building secure applications is an ongoing process involving continuous testing and adaptation to new security threats. As you further develop your Rust applications, consider diving deeper into established libraries and best practices to strengthen your security posture.

Implementing Token-Based Authentication (JWT)

In this chapter, we will explore how to implement JWT-based authentication in Rust, leveraging popular libraries and frameworks. By the end of this chapter, you'll have a foundational understanding of JWT concepts and the ability to create a simple web service that utilizes token-based authentication.

What is JWT?

JSON Web Tokens (JWT) are an open standard (RFC 7519) that defines a compact and self-contained way for securely transmitting information between parties as a JSON object. These tokens can be signed and optionally encrypted, ensuring that claims (or statements about data) can be trusted. Typically, JWTs consist of three parts:

Header: Contains information about how the token is encoded and what algorithm is used for signing it.

Payload: Contains the claims, which are statements about an entity (usually the user) and additional metadata.

Signature: Generated from the encoded header and payload, and a secret key. This is used to validate the authenticity of the token.

An important aspect of JWTs is that they are stateless; once issued, they do not require server-side storage. This allows for scalability and simplicity, making them particularly suited for modern microservices architectures.

Setting Up Our Rust Project

To get started, ensure you have Rust installed. If you haven't set up Rust yet, visit rustup.rs for installation instructions. Create a new Rust project using Cargo:

```bash
cargo new jwt_auth_example cd jwt_auth_example
```

Next, we will add our required dependencies to the `Cargo.toml` file. For JWT handling, we will use the `jsonwebtoken` library. We'll also need `actix-web` for building our web server. Edit `Cargo.toml` to include:

```toml [dependencies] actix-web = "4.0"
jsonwebtoken = { version = "8.0", features = ["serde"] } serde = { version = "1.0", features = ["derive"] } serde_json = "1.0"
```

Now, let's create our basic web server and define the necessary structures for our JWT implementation. ## Defining User and Claims Structures To represent our users and JWT claims, we will create corresponding structs. Create a new file named `models.rs`:

```rust
// models.rs
use serde::{Deserialize, Serialize};

#[derive(Debug, Serialize, Deserialize)] pub struct User {

pub username: String, pub password: String,

}

#[derive(Debug, Serialize, Deserialize)] pub struct Claims {
```

```rust
pub sub: String, // Subject (user identifier) pub exp:
usize, // Expiration time
}
```

Implementing JWT Creation and Validation

In our main file, we will write functions to create a JWT token and validate it. Create a new file named

`jwt.rs`:

```rust
// jwt.rs

use jsonwebtoken::{encode, decode, Header, Algorithm, DecodingKey, EncodingKey, Validation, errors::Error as JwtError};

use chrono::{Utc, Duration};

use crate::models::{Claims, User};

const SECRET: &[u8] = b"your_secret_key"; // Change to a secure random key in production. pub fn create_jwt(user: &User) -> Result<String, JwtError> {

let expiration = Utc::now() + Duration::hours(1); // Token valid for 1 hour let claims = Claims {

sub: user.username.clone(),

exp: expiration.timestamp() as usize,

};

encode(&Header::new(Algorithm::HS256),    &claims,
&EncodingKey::from_secret(SECRET))

}
```

```rust
pub fn validate_jwt(token: &str) -> Result<Claims,
JwtError> {
decode::<Claims>(token,
&DecodingKey::from_secret(SECRET),
&Validation::default()).map(|data| data.claims)
}
```
```

## Building the Web Server

Now let's set up our web server to handle user authentication. We'll create an endpoint for logging in that will issue a JWT upon valid credentials and an endpoint to access a protected resource.

Create or modify `main.rs`:

```rust
// main.rs

use actix_web::{web, App, HttpServer, HttpResponse,
Responder}; use serde_json::json;

use std::sync::Mutex;

mod models; mod jwt;

struct AppState {

users: Mutex<Vec<models::User>>,

}

async fn login(user: web::Json<models::User>, data:
web::Data<AppState>) -> impl Responder { let users =
data.users.lock().unwrap();
```
```

```rust
if users.iter().any(|u| u.username == user.username &&
u.password        ==        user.password)        {        match
jwt::create_jwt(&user) {

Ok(token)  =>  HttpResponse::Ok().json(json!({"token":
token})),                  Err(_)                    =>
HttpResponse::InternalServerError().finish(),

}

} else {

HttpResponse::Unauthorized().finish()

}

}

async fn protected_route(token: web::Header<String>) ->
impl Responder { match jwt::validate_jwt(&token.0) {

Ok(claims)                                           =>
HttpResponse::Ok().json(json!({"message":       "Access
granted!",    "user":    claims.sub})),    Err(_)    =>
HttpResponse::Unauthorized().finish(),

}

}

#[actix_web::main]

async fn main() -> std::io::Result<()> { let app_state =
AppState {

users: Mutex::new(vec![

models::User { username: "user1".to_string(), password:
"password".to_string()  },  models::User  {  username:
"user2".to_string(), password: "password".to_string() },
```

80

```
]),
};
HttpServer::new(move || { App::new()
.app_data(web::Data::new(app_state.clone()))
.route("/login", web::post().to(login))
.route("/protected", web::get().to(protected_route))
})
.bind("127.0.0.1:8080")?
.run()
.await
```

```
}
```

Testing the Implementation

To test the implementation, start your server using:

```bash cargo run
```

You can use tools like `curl` or any REST client to interact with the endpoints:

Login:

```bash
curl -X POST http://localhost:8080/login -H "Content-Type: application/json" -d '{"username": "user1", "password": "password"}'
```

```
```

If the credentials are correct, you will receive a JWT token in the response.

Access Protected Route:

Use the token received in the login response to access the protected route:

```bash
curl -X GET http://localhost:8080/protected -H "Authorization: Bearer <your_token>"
```

Replace `<your_token>` with the actual JWT token.

In this chapter, we explored how to implement JWT-based token authentication in a Rust web application using the `actix-web` framework. We created a basic user model, defined JWT claims, implemented the logic to create and validate tokens, and built a server that demonstrates login and protected routes.

By understanding and implementing JWTs in Rust, you have laid the groundwork for building robust and secure web applications. In the following chapters, we will explore more advanced topics, including user registration, roles and permissions, and integrating JWT with databases and other authentication mechanisms.

Role-Based Access Control in Rust Applications

This model allows developers to assign roles to users, which in turn dictates their access to resources within an application. In the context of Rust, a systems programming language known for its performance and memory safety features, implementing RBAC can lead to robust, secure web applications.

In this chapter, we will explore the concept of RBAC, its importance in web development, and how to implement it in a Rust-based application. We will cover the fundamental constructs of RBAC, how to define roles and permissions, and best practices for integrating RBAC into your Rust web application.

Understanding Role-Based Access Control ### What is RBAC?

RBAC is an access control method that assigns permissions to specific roles rather than to individual users. This abstraction simplifies user management, as users are granted roles that inherently possess specific permissions. For example, in a web application, you might have roles such as "Admin," "Editor," and "Viewer," each with different levels of access to resources.

Why Use RBAC?

Simplifies Management: Managing permissions at the role level streamlines user management, especially in large organizations where user roles can frequently change.

Improves Security: By enforcing least privilege access, RBAC helps to minimize the risk of unauthorized access to sensitive resources.

Scalable: As applications grow, updating the permissions in one location (the role itself) rather than for every individual user reduces overhead and potential errors.

Setting Up a Rust Web Application

To implement RBAC in a Rust web application, we'll start with a basic setup using the `actix-web` framework—one of the most popular web frameworks in Rust.

Project Setup

Create a New Rust Project:

```bash
cargo new rust_rb_webapp cd rust_rb_webapp
```

Add Dependencies: Open `Cargo.toml` and add the necessary dependencies.

```toml
[dependencies] actix-web = "4.0"

serde = { version = "1.0", features = ["derive"] } serde_json = "1.0"

jsonwebtoken = "8.0" # For handling JWTs
```

Define Roles and Permissions

To implement RBAC, we need a model to represent roles and permissions. Here's a simple example using enums and structs.

```rust
use serde::{Serialize, Deserialize};

#[derive(Serialize, Deserialize, Debug)] enum Role {

Admin, Editor, Viewer,
```

```
}
```

```rust
#[derive(Serialize, Deserialize, Debug)] struct User {

username: String, role: Role,

}
```

Middleware for RBAC

Middleware is a crucial part of web applications, allowing us to run code before controllers handle requests. We can create a middleware to check the user role against the required permissions.

```rust
use actix_web::{Error, HttpRequest, HttpResponse, Result}; use std::collections::HashMap;

async fn rbac_middleware(req: HttpRequest) -> Result<HttpResponse, Error> { let user: User = req.extensions().get::<User>().unwrap();


let permissions: HashMap<&'static str, Vec<Role>> = [ ("/admin", vec![Role::Admin]),

("/edit", vec![Role::Admin, Role::Editor]),

("/view", vec![Role::Admin, Role::Editor, Role::Viewer]),

].iter().cloned().collect();

let path = req.path();

if let Some(allowed_roles) = permissions.get(path) { if allowed_roles.contains(&user.role) {

return Ok(req.error_response(HttpResponse::Ok()));
```

```
} else {
return
Ok(req.error_response(HttpResponse::Forbidden()));
}
}
Ok(req.error_response(HttpResponse::NotFound()))
}
```
```

This middleware checks if the role of the user accessing the endpoint matches the required permissions for that endpoint.

### Integrating Roles in Endpoints

Next, we will modify our route handlers to include the RBAC middleware. Here's how you can set up simple endpoints.

```rust
use actix_web::{web, App, HttpServer};

#[actix_web::main]
async fn main() -> std::io::Result<()> {
HttpServer::new(|| {
App::new()
.route("/admin", web::get().to(admin_endpoint))
.route("/edit", web::get().to(edit_endpoint))
.route("/view", web::get().to(view_endpoint))
.wrap_fn(rbac_middleware) // Apply middleware here
```
```

```
})
.bind("127.0.0.1:8080")?
.run()
.await
}

async fn admin_endpoint() -> HttpResponse {
HttpResponse::Ok().body("Welcome, Admin!")
}

async fn edit_endpoint() -> HttpResponse {
HttpResponse::Ok().body("Welcome, Editor!")
}

async fn view_endpoint() -> HttpResponse {
HttpResponse::Ok().body("Welcome, Viewer!")
}
```
```

## Best Practices for Implementing RBAC

**Role Hierarchies**: Design roles with hierarchies where more privileged roles inherit permissions from less privileged roles to reduce complexity.

**Audit & Logging**: Implement logging to track access and changes to roles and permissions.

**Testing**: Rigorously test your RBAC implementation to ensure that access is enforced correctly across all routes.

**Documentation**: Maintain clear documentation of roles, permissions, and access policies within your
```

application to help onboard new developers.

Regular Reviews: Periodically review and update roles and permissions as the application evolves.

By leveraging Rust's type safety and performance features, along with a robust web framework like `actix- web`, developers can implement a secure and scalable RBAC system. As we have outlined in this chapter,

understanding the structure of roles and permissions, integrating them effectively into your application, and adhering to best practices is crucial for maintaining a secure application environment. As web applications become more complex, mastering RBAC in Rust will be an invaluable tool in your development toolkit.

Chapter 6: Database Integration

One of the key elements of modern web development is efficient database integration. In this chapter, we will explore various aspects of integrating databases into Rust web applications, including popular libraries, design patterns, and best practices.

6.1 Understanding the Basics of Database Integration

At its core, database integration involves connecting web applications with databases to store, retrieve, and manipulate data. Databases can be classified into two primary categories:

SQL Databases: These include relational databases like PostgreSQL, MySQL, and SQLite. SQL databases use structured schemas and provide ACID (Atomicity, Consistency, Isolation, Durability) properties, making them ideal for applications requiring complex queries and transactions.

NoSQL Databases: These databases, such as MongoDB and Redis, provide more flexibility in terms of data structures. They are often chosen for applications requiring scalability and high-speed data access.

In Rust, integrating with either type of database can be achieved through various libraries designed to simplify interaction with database systems.

6.2 Popular Rust Libraries for Database Integration

Rust has a rich ecosystem of libraries that facilitate database integration. Some of the most popular options include:

6.2.1 Diesel

[Diesel](https://diesel.rs/) is one of the most widely used ORM (Object-Relational Mapping) libraries in Rust. It provides a type-safe way to interact with SQL databases. With Diesel, developers can define their database schema using Rust types, leveraging compile-time checks to catch errors early in development.

Key Features:

Strong focus on type safety and compile-time checks.

Support for migrations to manage database schema changes.

Query builder that allows for expressive and dynamic SQL queries.

Example:

```rust
#[macro_use] extern crate diesel;

mod schema;

use diesel::prelude::*; use schema::users::dsl::*;

#[derive(Queryable)] struct User {

id: i32, name: String,


email: String,

}

fn    fetch_all_users(connection:    &PgConnection)    ->
QueryResult<Vec<User>>                                 {
users.load::<User>(connection)

}
```

6.2.2 SQLx

[SQLx](https://github.com/launchbadge/sqlx) is another versatile library for interacting with databases in Rust. Unlike Diesel, SQLx adopts an asynchronous approach and provides a lightweight, flexible interface. This library is perfect for applications that require non-blocking I/O operations.

Key Features:

Asynchronous support with `async/await`.

Compile-time verification of SQL queries.

Support for multiple database systems, including Postgres, MySQL, and SQLite.

Example:

```rust
use sqlx::PgPool;

async fn get_user(pool: &PgPool, user_id: i32) -> Result<User, sqlx::Error> { let user: User = sqlx::query_as("SELECT * FROM users WHERE id = $1")

.bind(user_id)

.fetch_one(pool)

.await?; Ok(user)

}
```

6.2.3 SeaORM

[SeaORM](https://www.sea-ql.org/SeaORM/) is a newer player in the Rust ORM ecosystem, emphasizing async capabilities. It is designed to work seamlessly with various databases and offers a lightweight and expressive API.

Key Features:

Fully asynchronous and compatible with async runtimes.

Provides an easy-to-use query builder.

Offers a strong type-safe schema and migrations.

Example:

```rust
use sea_orm::entity::*;

use sea_orm::DatabaseConnection;

async fn find_users(db: &DatabaseConnection) -> Result<Vec<User>, DbErr> { User::find().all(db).await

}
```

6.3 Best Practices for Database Integration

Integrating a database into a Rust web application requires following certain best practices to ensure maintainability and performance:

6.3.1 Use Connection Pooling

Creating a new database connection for every request can lead to performance bottlenecks. Instead, utilize connection pooling libraries like `r2d2` or support built into ORMs like SQLx to manage a pool of reusable connections.

6.3.2 Error Handling

Robust error handling is critical when dealing with database operations. Use enums or custom error types to categorize various errors (e.g., connection errors, query errors) and return meaningful messages to users when operations fail.

6.3.3 Employ Migrations

Database migrations are essential for managing schema changes over time. Using the migration features provided by ORM libraries helps keep track of schema changes and ensures compatibility across different versions of the application.

6.3.4 Asynchronous Programming

If your application is I/O-bound or requires handling multiple database queries simultaneously, consider leveraging Rust's asynchronous capabilities. This can vastly improve the responsiveness and scalability of your application.

6.3.5 Security Considerations

When integrating databases, always utilize prepared statements to safeguard against SQL injection attacks. Additionally, review access controls to limit the data exposure based on user roles.

By leveraging powerful libraries such as Diesel, SQLx, and SeaORM, developers can interact with both SQL and NoSQL databases with ease while benefiting from Rust's strong guarantees around memory safety and concurrency.

Connecting to Databases with Diesel and SQLx

Rust, known for its performance and safety, offers several libraries to facilitate database interactions, two of the most prominent being Diesel and SQLx. In this chapter, we will explore how to connect to databases using these libraries, highlight their unique features, and provide practical examples to help you understand their usage in real-world applications.

1. Understanding Diesel ### 1.1 What is Diesel?

Diesel is a powerful and efficient ORM (Object-Relational Mapping) library for Rust, which provides a safe and expressive way to interact with SQL databases. It is designed to be type-safe and aims to leverage Rust's compile-time guarantees to minimize runtime errors.

1.2 Getting Started with Diesel

To start using Diesel, you first need to add it to your `Cargo.toml` file:

```toml
[dependencies]
diesel = { version = "2.0", features = ["mysql", "r2d2"] }
dotenv = "0.15"
```

After specifying the dependencies, run `cargo build` to fetch them. ### 1.3 Setting Up the Database

Before you can interact with a database, you need to set it up. We'll use a MySQL database for this example. Ensure you have MySQL installed and running, then create a new database:

```sql
```

```
CREATE DATABASE my_database;
```

1.4 Creating the Database Connection

Next, create a `.env` file in your project root to store your database connection URL:

```
DATABASE_URL=mysql://username:password@localhost/my_database
```

Here's how to establish a connection in your Rust application:

```rust
use diesel::prelude::*; use dotenv::dotenv; use std::env;


fn establish_connection() -> MysqlConnection { dotenv().ok();

let database_url = env::var("DATABASE_URL").expect("DATABASE_URL must be set");
MysqlConnection::establish(&database_url).expect(&format!("Error connecting to {}", database_url))

}
```

2. Working with SQLx ### 2.1 What is SQLx?

SQLx is another powerful library for interacting with databases in Rust, but it distinguishes itself by being asynchronous and supporting multiple database backends like PostgreSQL, MySQL, and SQLite. It provides a more flexible approach for developers who prefer to write raw SQL queries.

2.2 Getting Started with SQLx

To use SQLx, you need to modify your `Cargo.toml` similarly:

```toml
[dependencies]
```

sqlx = { version = "0.5", features = ["mysql", "runtime-async-std"] } dotenv = "0.15"

```

```

Again, run `cargo build` to fetch the dependencies. ### 2.3 Setting Up the Database Connection

Just like we did in Diesel, we will use an environment variable for the database connection URL. The connection string syntax remains the same, but SQLx offers an async function to establish connections:

```rust
```

use sqlx::mysql::MySqlPoolOptions; use dotenv::dotenv;

use std::env;

async fn establish_connection() -> sqlx::Result<sqlx::Pool<sqlx::MySql>> { dotenv().ok();

let database_url = env::var("DATABASE_URL").expect("DATABASE_URL must be set"); MySqlPoolOptions::new()

.max_connections(5)

.connect(&database_url)

```
.await
}
```

3. Performing Basic CRUD Operations

Now that we can connect to our databases, let's perform some basic CRUD operations (Create, Read, Update, Delete) with both Diesel and SQLx.

3.1 Using Diesel for CRUD Operations

Creating a Record

Assuming we have a `users` table, we can define a Rust struct for it:

```rust
#[derive(Insertable)] #[table_name = "users"]
struct NewUser<'a> {

username: &'a str, email: &'a str,

}
```

Inserting a new user would look like this:

```rust
use diesel::insert_into;

fn create_user(conn: &MysqlConnection, username: &str, email: &str) { let new_user = NewUser { username, email };

insert_into(users::table)

.values(&new_user)
```

```
.execute(conn)
.expect("Error saving new user");
}
```

Reading Records

To fetch users, you may do the following:

```rust
use diesel::select;

fn get_users(conn: &MysqlConnection) -> Vec<User> {
use schema::users::dsl::*;


users.load::<User>(conn).expect("Error loading users")
}
```

Updating a Record

Updating a user's information is also straightforward:

```rust
fn update_user(conn: &MysqlConnection, user_id: i32,
new_email: &str) { use schema::users::dsl::{users, email};

diesel::update(users.find(user_id))
.set(email.eq(new_email))
.execute(conn)
.expect("Error updating user");
```

}
```

#### Deleting a Record

Finally, deleting a user can be accomplished by:

```rust
fn delete_user(conn: &MysqlConnection, user_id: i32) {
use schema::users::dsl::users;

diesel::delete(users.find(user_id))

.execute(conn)

.expect("Error deleting user");

}
```

3.2 Using SQLx for CRUD Operations

In SQLx, the pattern is quite similar, utilizing async/await features. #### Creating a Record

For creating records, your function will look like this:

```rust
use sqlx::query;

async fn create_user(pool: &sqlx::Pool<sqlx::MySql>, username: &str, email: &str) -> sqlx::Result<()> {
query("INSERT INTO users (username, email) VALUES (?, ?)")

.bind(username)

.bind(email)

.execute(pool)
```
```

```rust
.await?;
Ok(())
}
```

Reading Records

Reading records can be done as follows:

```rust
async fn get_users(pool: &sqlx::Pool<sqlx::MySql>) ->
sqlx::Result<Vec<User>> { let users = query_as::<_,
User>("SELECT * FROM users")
.fetch_all(pool)
.await?; Ok(users)
}
```

Updating a Record

Updating is accomplished similarly:

```rust
async fn update_user(pool: &sqlx::Pool<sqlx::MySql>,
user_id: i32, new_email: &str) -> sqlx::Result<()> {
query("UPDATE users SET email = ? WHERE id = ?")
.bind(new_email)
.bind(user_id)
.execute(pool)
```

.await?;

Ok(())

}

```

#### Deleting a Record

Finally, deleting a user would look like this:

```rust
async fn delete_user(pool: &sqlx::Pool<sqlx::MySql>,
user_id: i32) -> sqlx::Result<()> { query("DELETE FROM
users WHERE id = ?")

.bind(user_id)

.execute(pool)

.await?;

Ok(())

}
```

In this chapter, we examined two formidable Rust libraries, Diesel and SQLx, for connecting and interacting with databases in web development. Diesel's emphasis on type safety and ORM features allows for structured, safe database interactions, while SQLx's asynchronous capabilities enable high performance in I/O-bound applications.
```

Performing CRUD Operations in Rust

These operations represent the four essential functions that any persistent storage management system should effectively support. In the context of web development, CRUD operations form the backbone of any application that interacts with a database, enabling users to manage their data effectively.

Rust, known for its speed, safety, and concurrency capabilities, has become an attractive choice for web development. With frameworks such as Actix and Rocket, developers can build robust web applications that perform CRUD operations efficiently. This chapter focuses on implementing CRUD operations in a Rust web application and will guide you through each operation step by step.

Setting Up the Environment

Before diving into the implementation of CRUD operations, you need to ensure that your Rust development environment is set up correctly. Follow these steps:

Install Rust: If you haven't already, install Rust by following the instructions on the [official Rust website](https://www.rust-lang.org/).

Create a new project: Use Cargo, Rust's package manager, to create a new project:

```bash

cargo new rust_crud_app cd rust_crud_app

```

Add dependencies: Open the `Cargo.toml` file and include the necessary dependencies for web development and database interaction. For this chapter, we will use Actix-web for the web framework and Diesel for ORM and database handling:

```toml
[dependencies]
actix-web = "4.0"
diesel = { version = "2.0", features = ["r2d2", "postgres"] }
dotenv = "0.15"
serde = { version = "1.0", features = ["derive"] }
serde_json = "1.0"
```

Set up the database: We will use PostgreSQL for our database. Make sure you have it installed and running. Create a database named `rust_crud_db`.

Configuring Diesel

To set up Diesel for PostgreSQL, perform the following steps:

Install Diesel CLI: You can install Diesel CLI using Cargo:

```bash
cargo install diesel_cli --no-default-features --features postgres
```

Create a `.env` file: In the root of your project, create a `.env` file and add your database URL:

```plaintext
```

DATABASE_URL=postgres://user:password@localhost/rust_crud_db
```

**Run Diesel setup**: Initialize Diesel in your project:
```bash diesel setup
```

Create a migration: Generate a migration for a sample entity, such as `posts`:
```bash

diesel migration generate create_posts
```

Populate the generated migration files in `migrations/` to create a table:
```sql

-- up.sql

CREATE TABLE posts (

id SERIAL PRIMARY KEY, title VARCHAR NOT NULL,

content TEXT NOT NULL

);

-- down.sql

DROP TABLE posts;
```

Then run your migration:
```bash

```
diesel migration run
```
```

Implementing CRUD Operations ### 1. Create Operation

To handle the creation of a new post, you can create an endpoint in Actix-web.

```rust
use actix_web::{post, web, HttpResponse, HttpServer, App}; use diesel::prelude::*;

#[derive(Insertable, serde::Serialize)] #[table_name = "posts"]

struct NewPost { title: String, content: String,

}

#[post("/posts")]

async fn create_post(new_post: web::Json<NewPost>, pool: web::Data<DbPool>) -> HttpResponse { let conn = pool.get().expect("Could not get DB connection from pool");

diesel::insert_into(posts::table)

.values(&*new_post)

.execute(&conn)


.expect("Error saving new post");

HttpResponse::Created().finish()

}
```
```

```
```

2. Read Operation

To read posts, you can create a GET endpoint.

```rust
#[get("/posts")]
async fn get_posts(pool: web::Data<DbPool>) -> HttpResponse {

let conn = pool.get().expect("Could not get DB connection from pool");

let results = posts::table

.load::<Post>(&conn)

.expect("Error loading posts");

HttpResponse::Ok().json(results)

}
```

3. Update Operation

The update operation requires a PATCH endpoint to modify an existing post.

```rust
#[patch("/posts/{id}")]
async fn update_post(id: web::Path<i32>, updated_post: web::Json<NewPost>, pool: web::Data<DbPool>) -

> HttpResponse {

let conn = pool.get().expect("Could not get DB connection from pool");

diesel::update(posts::table.find(&id))

.set(&*updated_post)
```

```
.execute(&conn)
.expect("Error updating post");
HttpResponse::Ok().finish()
}
```

4. Delete Operation

Finally, create an endpoint to delete a post.

```rust
#[delete("/posts/{id}")]
async fn delete_post(id: web::Path<i32>, pool: web::Data<DbPool>) -> HttpResponse { let conn = pool.get().expect("Could not get DB connection from pool");
diesel::delete(posts::table.find(&id))
.execute(&conn)
.expect("Error deleting post");


HttpResponse::NoContent().finish()
}
```

Setting Up the Main Function

Once the CRUD operations are ready, tie them together in your main function.

```rust
use actix_web::{web, App, HttpServer};
```

```rust
#[actix_web::main]
async fn main() -> std::io::Result<()> {
let pool = establish_connection(); // Implement
connection establishment
HttpServer::new(move || { App::new()
.app_data(web::Data::new(pool.clone()))
.service(create_post)
.service(get_posts)
.service(update_post)
.service(delete_post)
})
.bind("127.0.0.1:8080")?
.run()
.await
}
```
```

We set up a simple web application that allows users to create, read, update, and delete posts in a PostgreSQL database. Rust's powerful features, combined with its safety guarantees, make it an excellent choice for web development.
```

Chapter 7: Advanced Web Development Techniques

In this chapter, we will explore advanced techniques in Rust web development, focusing on aspects such as asynchronous programming, web frameworks, APIs, security practices, and deployment strategies. We aim to provide you with a robust understanding of how to leverage Rust's unique features to build efficient, maintainable, and secure web applications.

7.1 Rust Web Frameworks Overview

Rust offers several web frameworks you can use to build web applications. Each framework has its strengths and trade-offs, allowing developers to choose based on specific project requirements. Here's a brief overview of some of the most popular Rust web frameworks:

Actix Web: A powerful, actor-based web framework that leverages Rust's asynchronous capabilities. It is known for high performance and ease of use.

Rocket: A web framework that prioritizes ease of development and type safety. It integrates seamlessly with Rust's type system, reducing runtime errors while providing an expressive syntax.

Warp: A lightweight, composable web framework built on top of the Tokio asynchronous runtime. Warp emphasizes the use of filters, making it easy to build complex routes and middleware.

Understanding the characteristics and advantages of these frameworks will help you choose the right tool for your project.

7.2 Asynchronous Programming with Rust

Asynchronous programming is crucial in web development, especially for applications serving multiple clients simultaneously. Rust's async features help manage these scenarios efficiently. Here's how you can effectively use async capabilities in your web applications:

7.2.1 Introduction to Async/Await

Rust introduced the `async`/`await` syntax, allowing you to write asynchronous code that looks synchronous. This transformation improves readability and maintainability. Consider the following example:

```rust
use tokio::time;

async fn fetch_data() -> String {

// Simulate an asynchronous operation
time::sleep(time::Duration::from_secs(1)).await; "Data fetched".to_string()

}
```

You can execute this asynchronous function in a web server handler to avoid blocking the thread. ### 7.2.2 Using Tokio

To harness the power of asynchronous programming, using an asynchronous runtime such as Tokio is essential. With Tokio, you can create non-blocking applications that scale efficiently:

```rust
use actix_web::{web, App, HttpServer, Responder};

async fn index() -> impl Responder {

let data = fetch_data().await; // Awaiting the asynchronous function format!("Response: {}", data)

}

#[tokio::main]

async fn main() -> std::io::Result<()> {
HttpServer::new(|| {

App::new().route("/", web::get().to(index))

})

.bind("127.0.0.1:8080")?

.run()

.await

}
```

In this example, the server handles requests asynchronously, allowing it to handle many requests concurrently.

7.3 Building RESTful APIs in Rust

Creating a performant and secure RESTful API is a common requirement in modern applications. Rust provides excellent tools to accomplish this:

7.3.1 Defining Routes and Handlers

Utilizing web frameworks like Rocket or Actix, you can define routes efficiently. Here's a basic example using Actix Web:

```rust
use actix_web::{get, post, web, App, HttpServer, HttpResponse};

// Define a handler for GET requests #[get("/items/{id}")]
async fn get_item(web::Path(id): web::Path<u32>) -> HttpResponse { HttpResponse::Ok().body(format!("Item ID: {}", id))
}

// Define a handler for POST requests #[post("/items")]
async fn create_item(item: web::Json<Item>) -> HttpResponse {
// Logic to create item HttpResponse::Created().finish()
}
```

7.3.2 Serializing and Deserializing Data

Rust's Serde library simplifies data serialization and deserialization, which is essential for API development. You can easily convert Rust structs to JSON and vice versa:

```rust
```

```
use serde::{Deserialize, Serialize};
#[derive(Serialize, Deserialize)] struct Item {
id: u32, name: String,
}
```
` ` `

By integrating Serde, you ensure robust handling of data formats, making your APIs more flexible. ## 7.4 Security Best Practices

When you develop web applications, security should be paramount. Rust's memory safety features reduce many classes of vulnerabilities, but there are additional practices to consider:

7.4.1 Input Validation and Sanitization

Always validate and sanitize user inputs to protect against injection attacks. Utilizing libraries like

`validator` can streamline this process:

` ` `rust

```
use validator::Validate;
#[derive(Validate)] struct User {
#[validate(length(min = 1))] username: String,
}
```
` ` `

7.4.2 Authentication and Authorization

Implementing robust authentication methods, such as OAuth2 or JWT, is crucial. Libraries like `jsonwebtoken` can help create and verify JWT tokens to secure your APIs.

```rust
use jsonwebtoken::{encode, decode, Header, Validation};

fn create_jwt(user_id: &str) -> String {

let token = encode(&Header::default(), &user_id, &secret_key).unwrap(); token

}
```

7.5 Deployment Strategies

Finally, once your application is built, you need to consider deployment. Below are some popular strategies to deploy Rust web applications:

7.5.1 Containerization with Docker

Docker can simplify the deployment process. You can create a Dockerfile for your Rust application like this:

```Dockerfile
FROM rust:1.60 as builder WORKDIR /usr/src/myapp COPY . .

RUN cargo install --path .

FROM debian:buster-slim

COPY --from=builder /usr/local/cargo/bin/myapp /usr/local/bin/myapp CMD ["myapp"]
```

7.5.2 Continuous Integration and Continuous Deployment (CI/CD)

Implementing CI/CD pipelines with tools like GitHub Actions or GitLab CI can enhance your deployment process, automate testing, and ensure code quality.

7.5.3 Hosting Options

When hosting Rust web applications, consider platforms like Heroku, DigitalOcean, or AWS, which can handle the deployment and scaling of your app effectively.

In this chapter, we've explored the advanced facets of web development using Rust, focusing on asynchronous programming, building RESTful APIs, implementing security best practices, and efficient deployment strategies. By embracing these techniques, you can leverage Rust's capabilities to craft high-performance and secure web applications that stand the test of modern demands. As you continue to grow your skills in Rust, remember that the community is a valuable resource—keep learning, experimenting, and contributing!

Middleware in Actix and Rocket for Custom Logic

This chapter will explore how to implement custom middleware in two prominent Rust web frameworks—Actix and Rocket. By the end, you will understand how to create middleware that can be tailored for your specific logic, enhancing the versatility and maintainability of your Rust applications.

1. Understanding Middleware

Middleware functions are critical to the request-response cycle in web applications. They allow developers to intercept requests as they come in, perform necessary operations, and pass control to the next middleware or the final handler. In the context of Rust web frameworks, middleware acts as an interface for injecting custom logic that can modify requests or responses, handle errors, and manage session state without cluttering the application's main logic.

2. Middleware in Actix ### 2.1 What is Actix?

Actix is a powerful, pragmatic, and extremely fast web framework for Rust. Its actor-based model allows for efficient asynchronous operations, making it suitable for building scalable web applications.

2.2 Creating Middleware in Actix

In Actix, middleware is created by implementing the `Middleware` trait. Below, we'll walk through the creation of a simple logging middleware.

2.2.1 Example: Logging Middleware

Set Up Dependencies: In your `Cargo.toml`, include dependencies for Actix Web.

```toml [dependencies] actix-web = "4"

env_logger = "0.9"
```

Implement the Middleware:

```rust

116
```

```rust
use actix_web::{web, App, HttpServer, HttpResponse, middleware::Middleware, Error}; use std::time::Instant;

pub struct LoggingMiddleware;

impl<S> Middleware<S> for LoggingMiddleware {

fn call(&self, req: ServiceRequest, next: &S) -> Result<HttpResponse, Error> { let start_time = Instant::now();

let response = next.call(req)?;

let duration = start_time.elapsed(); println!("Request took: {:?}", duration);


Ok(response)
}
}
```

Register the Middleware:
```rust
#[actix_web::main]
async fn main() -> std::io::Result<()> { env_logger::init();

HttpServer::new(|| { App::new()

.wrap(LoggingMiddleware) // register the middleware

.route("/", web::get().to(|| async { HttpResponse::Ok().body("Hello, Actix") }))

})

.bind("127.0.0.1:8080")?

.run()
```

```
.await

}
```
` ` `

2.3 Testing Your Middleware

Send a request to your Actix server and observe the logs.
The middleware should log the time taken for each
request processed. This basic example illustrates how
middleware can abstract away repetitive logic so that it
can be reused across different endpoints.

3. Middleware in Rocket ### 3.1 What is Rocket?

Rocket is another popular web framework in Rust, known
for its type safety and easy-to-use API. Rocket focuses on
developer productivity and is ideal for building web
applications quickly.

3.2 Creating Middleware in Rocket

Jetting off from Actix, Rocket uses a slightly different
approach to middleware. In Rocket, you typically utilize
request guards and fairings.

3.2.1 Example: Custom Fairing for Logging

Set Up Dependencies:

In your `Cargo.toml`, include Rocket dependencies.

` ` `toml [dependencies]

rocket = { version = "0.5", features = ["full"] }
` ` `

Implement the Fairing:

```rust
use rocket::{self, fairing::{Fairing, Info, Kind}, Request,
Response}; use std::time::Instant;

struct Logger;

#[rocket::async_trait] impl Fairing for Logger {

fn info(&self) -> Info { Info {

name: "Request Logger",

kind: Kind::Ignite | Kind::Response,

}

}

async fn on_request(&self, request: &mut Request<'_>) {
let        start_time        =        Instant::now();
request.local_cache_mut(|| start_time);

}

async fn on_response(&self, _: &Request<'_>, response:
&mut  Response<'_>)  {  if  let  Some(start_time)  =
response.request().local_cache::<Instant>() {

let            duration            =
Instant::now().duration_since(*start_time);
println!("Request took: {:?}", duration);

}

}

}
```

Register the Fairing:

```rust
#[rocket::main]
async fn main() -> Result<(), rocket::Error> {
    rocket::build()
    .attach(Logger)
    .mount("/", routes![index])
    .launch()
    .await
}

#[get("/")]
fn index() -> &'static str { "Hello, Rocket!"
}
```

3.3 Testing Your Fairing

Just like the Actix example, you can test the Rocket application and observe the console output for each request. You should be able to see how long each request takes to process.

4. Customizing Middleware Logic

Both Actix and Rocket allow for extensive customization of middleware. You may include functionalities such as:

Authentication and Authorization: Control access to certain routes based on user roles or tokens.

Error Handling: Intercept errors globally and provide custom responses.

Session Management: Manage user sessions efficiently using middleware logic.

Request Validation: Validate incoming requests for certain parameters or formats before processing them further.

Middleware in Actix and Rocket is fundamental for implementing custom logic in your Rust applications. Whether you choose Actix's flexible middleware pattern or Rocket's fairing system, both frameworks provide powerful tools for enhancing your application with reusable and maintainable logic. As you progress with Rust programming, mastering middleware will enable you to build sophisticated, efficient, and well- structured web applications tailored to your needs.

Handling File Uploads and Downloads

In this chapter, we will cover how to implement file uploads and downloads in Rust web applications, using web frameworks such as Actix Web and Rocket. We will walk through the necessary tools, libraries, and best practices that help ensure secure and efficient file handling.

Setting Up Your Rust Environment for Web Development

Before diving into file uploads and downloads, it is essential to set up your Rust environment. Ensure that you have installed Rust through `rustup`, which is the recommended way to manage Rust versions and associated tools.

Install Rust: If you haven't installed Rust yet, run:

```bash
```

```
curl --proto '=https' --tlsv1.2 -sSf https://sh.rustup.rs | sh
```

Create a New Project: Initialize a new Rust project using Cargo:

```bash
cargo    new    file_upload_download_example    cd
file_upload_download_example
```

Add Dependencies: For web development, we need some crates (libraries). In your `Cargo.toml`, add:

```toml
[dependencies]

actix-web = "4.0" # For handling web requests actix-files
= "0.6" # For serving files

serde = { version = "1.0", features = ["derive"] } # For
JSON serialization tokio = { version = "1", features =
["full"] }     # Async runtimes
```

Handling File Uploads

1. Building the Upload Endpoint

To create a route that accepts file uploads, we can utilize Actix Web. Below is an example of how to set up an upload endpoint.

```rust
use actix_web::{web, App, HttpServer, HttpResponse};
use actix_multipart::Multipart;

use futures::stream::StreamExt; use std::fs::File;
```

```rust
use std::io::Write;

async fn upload_file(mut payload: Multipart) ->
Result<HttpResponse, actix_web::Error> { while let
Ok(Some(mut field)) = payload.next().await {

let filename = field

.content_disposition()

.get_file_name()

.unwrap_or("file.bin");

let filepath = format!("./uploads/{}", filename); let mut f =
File::create(filepath).unwrap();

// Stream the file content to the newly created file while let
Some(chunk) = field.next().await {

let data = chunk?; f.write_all(&data)?;

}

}

Ok(HttpResponse::Ok().body("File                    uploaded
successfully"))

}

#[actix_web::main]

async fn main() -> std::io::Result<()> {
HttpServer::new(|| {

App::new()

.route("/upload", web::post().to(upload_file))

})

.bind("127.0.0.1:8080")?
```

.run()

.await

}

```

### 2. Testing the Upload Endpoint

To test the upload functionality, you can use tools like `curl` or Postman. Here's how to do it with `curl` from the command line:

```bash
curl          -F          "file=@path_to_your_file"
http://localhost:8080/upload
```

3. Security Considerations

When handling file uploads, it is vital to enforce certain security practices:

Sanitize Filenames: Avoid directly using filenames from users to prevent path traversal attacks. Consider using a UUID or hash as a filename.

Limit File Types: Restrict the types of files that can be uploaded by checking the MIME type.

Limit File Size: Set a maximum allowable file size to prevent denial-of-service attacks involving large files.

Handling File Downloads

After uploading files, users often need the ability to download them. Below is an example of how to set up an endpoint for downloading files in Actix Web.
```

1. Building the Download Endpoint

To create a file download endpoint, you can use Actix's built-in file serving capabilities.

```rust
use actix_files::NamedFile; use std::path::Path;

async fn download_file(file_name: web::Path<String>) ->
Result<NamedFile, actix_web::Error> { let file_path =
Path::new("./uploads/").join(&*file_name);

Ok(NamedFile::open(file_path)?)
}
// Inside main function's `App` definition:

App::new()

.route("/download/{file_name}",
web::get().to(download_file))
```

2. Testing the Download Endpoint

You can test this endpoint using a web browser or a command-line tool like `curl`:

```bash
curl -O http://localhost:8080/download/file.bin
```

3. Security Considerations

Similar to uploads, it's essential to apply security practices in file downloads:

Validate File Existence: Always check that the file

exists and is accessible to the server before serving.

Restrict Downloadable Files: Implement checks to ensure users can only download files they are permitted to access.

By leveraging the capabilities of frameworks like Actix Web, developers can build robust applications that facilitate user interactions involving file management. As you implement these features, always keep security in mind—protect both your users and your application. In the next chapter, we will explore more about database interactions and how to persist uploaded file metadata in a persistent store.

Chapter 8: Asynchronous Programming in Rust

In the realm of web development, Rust's unique characteristics, including its safety, speed, and concurrency features, make it a powerful candidate. This chapter delves into asynchronous programming in Rust, particularly in the context of web development, exploring its principles, frameworks, and practical applications.

8.1 Understanding Asynchronous Programming

Asynchronous programming allows developers to write non-blocking code, meaning that a program can initiate a task and continue executing other tasks while waiting for the initial task to complete. This is especially beneficial in web development, where applications often need to handle multiple requests simultaneously without compromising performance.

8.1.1 The Need for Asynchronous Programming

In conventional (synchronous) programming, a function executes completely before moving on to the next line of code. This can lead to inefficiencies, especially in I/O-bound operations such as network requests, file system access, or database queries. If one task blocks execution, users face delays, resulting in a poor experience. Asynchronous programming solves this by allowing tasks to run concurrently, utilizing the time spent waiting for I/O operations to kick off other tasks.

8.1.2 Concepts and Terminology

To effectively work with asynchronous programming in Rust, it's crucial to understand some key concepts:

Futures: A `Future` in Rust is an abstraction representing a value that may be available at some point. It's a placeholder for the result of a computation that hasn't completed yet.

Async and Await: Rust provides the `async fn` syntax to define asynchronous functions and the

`await` keyword to yield control until a Future is ready. This syntax allows developers to write asynchronous code that looks similar to synchronous code.

Executors: An executor is responsible for polling Futures to drive them to completion. This can be part of a runtime (like Tokio or async-std), which manages scheduling and executing asynchronous tasks.

8.2 Asynchronous Libraries in Rust

Rust has a vibrant ecosystem of libraries and frameworks that facilitate asynchronous programming. Two of the most prominent runtime libraries are Tokio and async-std.

8.2.1 Tokio

Tokio is a standalone, asynchronous runtime that provides essential building blocks for writing network applications. Built on top of Futures and Streams, Tokio allows developers to leverage Rust's powerful concurrency capabilities seamlessly.

Example: Creating a Simple Web Server with Tokio

```rust
use tokio::net::TcpListener;
```

```rust
use tokio::prelude::*;

#[tokio::main]

async fn main() -> std::io::Result<()> {

let listener = TcpListener::bind("127.0.0.1:8080").await?;
loop {

let     (socket,     _)     =     listener.accept().await?;
tokio::spawn(async move {

// Handle the socket.

});

}

}
```

In this example, we create a TCP listener on port 8080. Each accepted socket is handled in an asynchronous task using `tokio::spawn`, allowing multiple connections to be processed concurrently.

8.2.2 async-std

Another popular option for asynchronous programming in Rust is async-std. Similar to the standard library, async-std provides asynchronous versions of standard library types.

Example: Using async-std to Read from a File

```rust
use async_std::fs::File;

use async_std::io::prelude::*;

#[async_std::main]
```

```
async fn main() -> std::io::Result<()> {
```

let mut file = File::open("hello.txt").await?; let mut contents = String::new(); file.read_to_string(&mut contents).await?; println!("{}", contents);

Ok(())

}

```

In this snippet, we read a file asynchronously, demonstrating how easy it is to integrate async functionality into traditional file operations.

## 8.3 Building a Web Application with Actix Web

Actix Web is another powerful framework for building web applications in Rust. It supports asynchronous programming out of the box and leverages Actix, an actor framework for Rust.

### 8.3.1 Setting Up an Actix Web Project

To start, add Actix dependencies to `Cargo.toml`:

```toml [dependencies] actix-web = "4.0"
```

8.3.2 Creating a Simple Web Server

Now let's create a basic HTTP server using Actix Web:

```rust
use actix_web::{web, App, HttpServer, Responder};

async fn greet() -> impl Responder { "Hello, world!"

}
```
```

```
#[actix_web::main]

async fn main() -> std::io::Result<()> {
HttpServer::new(|| {

App::new().route("/", web::get().to(greet))

})

.bind("127.0.0.1:8080")?

.run()

.await

}
```
```

Here, we define a simple HTTP server that responds with "Hello, world!" to GET requests on the root route. The server is straightforward to scale and adapt to more complex routing and middleware configurations.

## 8.4 Error Handling in Asynchronous Code

Error handling in asynchronous programming can sometimes be more complex than in synchronous code. Since Futures can fail in various ways, implementing effective error handling strategies is crucial.

### 8.4.1 Using Result and Option Types

Rust's `Result` and `Option` types are essential for capturing the success or failure of asynchronous operations. Here's an example that incorporates error handling in an async function:

```rust

async fn process_data(data: Option<&str>) ->
```
```

```
Result<String, String> { match data {

Some(value) => Ok(format!("Processed: {}", value)), None
=> Err("No data provided".into()),

}

}
```
` ` `

This function takes an optional string and returns a Result, encapsulating potential errors elegantly.

With a solid understanding of Futures, async/await syntax, and frameworks like Tokio, async-std, and Actix Web, you can leverage Rust's features to handle concurrency effectively.

Introduction to Async/Await for Web Applications

Traditional synchronous programming models often lead to inefficient use of resources, as threads are frequently blocked while waiting for external operations to complete. In contrast, asynchronous programming allows developers to write non-blocking code, improving the scalability and responsiveness of applications.

Rust, known for its memory safety and zero-cost abstractions, has embraced the async paradigm, providing robust tools for writing asynchronous code. The introduction of the async/await syntax has made it significantly easier to write and understand asynchronous code in Rust. This chapter serves as an introduction to async/await in Rust, particularly in the context of web applications.

1.2 Why Async/Await?

The async/await syntax allows developers to write asynchronous code that looks like synchronous code, making it far more readable and maintainable. This stylistic improvement addresses a common critique of earlier asynchronous programming patterns, where callback hell or excessive state management could render code convoluted and difficult to follow.

Key Benefits of Async/Await:

Improved Readability: Async/await allows developers to write sequential code without explicitly managing callbacks, making the flow of logic easier to understand.

Efficient Resource Usage: By using async programming, applications can handle many concurrent tasks with fewer threads, leading to lower memory overhead.

Native Integration with Rust's Safety Features: Rust's ownership system and borrowing rules apply to async functions, ensuring that code remains safe from data races and memory leaks.

1.3 Async/Await in Rust

Rust provides built-in support for asynchronous programming through the `async` and `await` keywords, which were stabilized in version 1.39. This feature allows developers to define functions that return `Future` types, which represent values that may not be immediately available.

Defining an Async Function

An async function in Rust can be defined using the `async fn` syntax. Here's a simple example:

```rust
async fn fetch_data() -> String {
// Simulate an async operation (e.g., a network request)
"data".to_string()
}
```

When calling an async function, it does not execute immediately. Instead, it returns a `Future`. The actual execution happens when the future is awaited:

```rust
let result = fetch_data().await;
```

The Role of Executors

To run async functions, we need an executor, a runtime that drives the execution of futures. The most common executor in Rust is provided by the `tokio` and `async-std` libraries. These libraries not only provide the executor but also include additional utilities such as timers, I/O operations, and more.

Example of an Async Web Request

Here's a more concrete example, demonstrating a simple asynchronous HTTP GET request using the

`reqwest` crate along with `tokio`:

```rust
use reqwest::Error;

#[tokio::main]
async fn main() -> Result<(), Error> {
    let response = reqwest::get("https://api.example.com/data")
        .await?
        .text()
        .await?;
    println!("Response: {}", response); Ok(())
}
```

In this example, we use `tokio::main` to define the main entry point of the program, allowing the async context to be established. The `reqwest::get` function performs an asynchronous HTTP GET request and returns a `Future`, which we await to get the response.

1.4 Best Practices for Using Async/Await

When writing asynchronous code in Rust, several best practices can help ensure efficient and maintainable applications:

Avoid Blocking Calls: If you need to perform blocking operations (like file I/O or CPU-bound tasks), consider using dedicated threads or spawning a blocking task. Blocking an async task can hinder performance.

Use the Right Executor: Choose an executor from

libraries like `tokio` or `async-std` that fits your application's needs, and be familiar with their features and limitations.

Error Handling: Use the `Result` and `?` operator for graceful error handling in your async functions, keeping the code clean and maintaining the control flow.

The introduction of async/await in Rust has opened up new avenues for writing efficient and expressive code in web applications. By leveraging this powerful approach, developers can create responsive and high- performance services that scale seamlessly. As we explore more advanced topics and patterns in subsequent chapters, having a solid understanding of async and await concepts will become crucial for building robust web applications in Rust.

Optimizing Performance with Async Rust

Rust, a systems programming language renowned for its memory safety and concurrency capabilities, offers robust support for asynchronous programming. This chapter explores how we can leverage Rust's async features to optimize performance in web development, enhancing responsiveness, scalability, and overall user experience.

Understanding Async Programming ### The Need for Asynchrony

In traditional synchronous programming models, each operation is performed in sequence, which can lead to inefficiencies, especially when dealing with IO-bound tasks, such as network requests or file operations.

With the rise of web applications that rely heavily on real-time data and user interactions, non-blocking operations become essential. Asynchronous programming allows developers to write code that can perform tasks concurrently, improving throughput and responsiveness.

Rust's Approach to Async

Rust provides an async/await syntax that simplifies asynchronous programming. This model allows developers to write code that looks synchronous while performing tasks asynchronously. The core of Rust's asynchronous programming model is the `Future` trait, which represents a value that may not be immediately available but will be resolved in the future. The `async` keyword transforms functions into non- blocking counterparts, and `await` is used to yield control until the `Future` is resolved.

Getting Started with Async Rust ### Setting Up Your Environment

To begin developing web applications in Rust, you will need to set up your environment:

Install Rust: Use the Rustup tool to install Rust, which ensures that you have the latest stable version.

```bash
curl --proto '=https' --tlsv1.2 -sSf https://sh.rustup.rs | sh
```

Choose a Framework: Several frameworks facilitate

137

async web development in Rust, the most notable being Actix, Rocket, and Warp. For this chapter, we'll focus on Warp, a minimal and composable web framework that uses Tokio for asynchronous runtime.

Add Dependencies: Update your `Cargo.toml` file to include necessary dependencies for async development:

```toml
[dependencies] warp = "0.3"

tokio = { version = "1", features = ["full"] }
```

Building the First Async Web Application

Let's dive into a simple example of creating an async web server using Warp.

```rust
use warp::Filter;

#[tokio::main] async fn main() {

// Define a route

let hello = warp::path!("hello" / String)

.map(|name| format!("Hello, {}!", name));

// Start the server

warp::serve(hello).run(([127, 0, 0, 1], 3030)).await;

}
```

In this code, we define a route that responds with a greeting message when accessed. The `#[tokio::main]` attribute indicates that the `main` function is an asynchronous entry point that runs the Tokio runtime, enabling the asynchronous server to handle requests concurrently.

Performance Optimization Techniques ### Efficient Resource Management

One of the key benefits of using async Rust is efficient resource management. To optimize performance:

Limit Blocking Operations: Avoid blocking calls in your async code. For example, use asynchronous versions of libraries (e.g., `tokio` for IO operations).

Connection Pooling: When working with databases or external services, utilize connection pooling. The `sqlx` library, for instance, supports async database connections that can optimize the performance of database queries.

Use Streaming: For large amounts of data, consider using streaming APIs. Warp supports streaming responses, enabling efficient handling of large datasets without consuming excessive memory.

Load Balancing and Scalability

Async Rust excels in scenarios requiring high concurrency, making load balancing and horizontal scalability straightforward.

Horizontal Scaling: Deploying multiple instances of your Rust application can take advantage of multi-core systems. Using container orchestration tools like Kubernetes can help manage these instances efficiently.

Load Testing: To optimize performance, load testing is essential. Tools like Apache Bench (ab), k6, or locust can simulate traffic to identify bottlenecks and ensure that your application can handle the expected load.

Handling Errors Gracefully

Errors can have a significant impact on user experience. Asynchronous applications, due to their concurrent nature, require careful handling of errors.

Result Types: Always handle potential errors by using Rust's `Result` type. Using the `?` operator can help propagate errors gracefully, enhancing the error-handling mechanism.

Custom Error Responses: Design custom error handling filters in Warp to return consistent error responses to clients. This ensures that clients receive useful information and enhances the user experience.

By embracing Rust's async capabilities, leveraging frameworks like Warp, and applying best practices for resource management and scalability, developers can create responsive and efficient web applications. As the landscape of web development continues to evolve, mastering async Rust can provide a competitive edge, enabling the creation of high-performance, scalable, and robust web services.

Chapter 9: Error Handling in Rust Web Applications

Rust, with its unique ownership model and focus on safety, offers powerful tools that can significantly enhance error management. In this chapter, we will explore various strategies for handling errors in Rust web applications, diving into both the standard library's features and community-provided crates that elevate error handling to a new level.

9.1 Understanding Errors in Rust

In Rust, errors are categorized mainly into two types: **recoverable** and **unrecoverable** errors. Recoverable errors are those which a program can handle gracefully, allowing for a fallback path or a retry mechanism. Unrecoverable errors, on the other hand, signal a condition that a program cannot cope with, leading to a panic and termination of the program.

9.1.1 Recoverable Errors

Recoverable errors are typically represented by the `Result` type, which is an enum defined as:

```rust
enum Result<T, E> {
    Ok(T),
    Err(E),
}
```

This structure allows developers to explicitly handle different outcomes of function calls. For instance, when working with file I/O or database queries, the function can return a `Result`, enabling the caller to choose how to respond to failure.

9.1.2 Unrecoverable Errors

Unrecoverable errors are indicated through the `panic!` macro, which immediately halts the program execution. While panicking can be appropriate in some scenarios (like when encountering bugs that should never occur), it is generally advised to use it sparingly in a web application context where uptime and user experience are critical.

9.2 Error Handling Strategies in Web Applications

Rust provides various mechanisms to handle errors effectively in web applications. We'll discuss some common strategies that can be employed.

9.2.1 Using the `Result` Type

Utilizing the `Result` type is paramount in building a web service. It allows you to represent outcomes gracefully. For example, when fetching data from a database, you might return a `Result`:

```rust
fn get_user(user_id: i32) -> Result<User, DatabaseError> {
// Function logic to fetch user
}
```

This way, the caller can handle the `Ok(User)` or `Err(DatabaseError)` gracefully, allowing the application to respond to the user appropriately.

9.2.2 Custom Error Types

Creating custom error types provides more context about the errors occurring in your application. This can be done by defining your own enums or structs implementing the `std::error::Error` trait. Here's a simple example:

```rust
#[derive(Debug)]

pub enum MyAppError { DatabaseError(DatabaseError),
InvalidInputError(String),

}

impl std::fmt::Display for MyAppError {

fn fmt(&self, f: &mut std::fmt::Formatter<'_>) -> std::fmt::Result { write!(f, "{:?}", self)

}

}

impl std::error::Error for MyAppError {}
```

We can then propagate these custom errors up the call chain, making it easier to handle them meaningfully in the HTTP response layer.

9.2.3 Leveraging the `anyhow` and `thiserror` Crates

The Rust ecosystem provides crates like `anyhow` and `thiserror` that simplify error management:

- **`anyhow`**: This crate provides a convenient way to propagate errors without having to define custom error types for every component of your application. It allows for easy conversion of various error types to a dynamic error type.

Example:

```rust
use anyhow::{Context, Result};

fn example_function() -> Result<()> {

let user = get_user(123).context("Failed to fetch user")?;

// Continue with logic Ok(())

}
```

- **`thiserror`**: This crate offers a way to define custom error types with minimal boilerplate. By deriving `thiserror::Error`, you can succinctly declare errors with helpful context.

Example:

```rust
use thiserror::Error;

#[derive(Debug, Error)] pub enum MyAppError {

#[error("database error: {0}")] DatabaseError(#[from] DatabaseError),    #[error("invalid    input:    {0}")] InvalidInputError(String),

}
```

9.3 Implementing Error Handling in Web Frameworks

Using frameworks such as Actix Web or Rocket, you can integrate error handling directly into your request

144

handlers.

9.3.1 Actix Web Example

In Actix Web, a common pattern for error handling can be established in your request handlers:

```rust
use actix_web::{web, HttpResponse, Responder}; use thiserror::Error;

#[derive(Debug, Error)] pub enum ApiError {

#[error("internal server error")] Internal,

#[error("not found")] NotFound,

}

async fn handler() -> Result<impl Responder, ApiError> {
let user = get_user(1).map_err(|_| ApiError::NotFound)?;
Ok(HttpResponse::Ok().json(user))

}
```

By mapping specific errors to your custom error type, you can maintain a clear error response structure. ### 9.3.2 Rocket Example

In Rocket, you define a catch-all error handler that captures specific errors and formats them into a JSON response:

```rust #[catch(404)]

fn not_found() -> Json<ErrorResponse> {

Json(ErrorResponse { message: "Resource not found".into() })
```

```
}
#[catch(500)]
fn    internal_error()    ->    Json<ErrorResponse>    {
Json(ErrorResponse    {    message:    "Internal    server
error".into() })
}
```
```

Utilizing catchable errors in Rocket allows a centralized
approach to error reporting. ## 9.4 Logging and
Monitoring

When dealing with errors in web applications, logging
becomes crucial. Libraries such as `log` and `tracing`
provide powerful tools for defining logs at various severity
levels. Logging errors allows developers to monitor
systems in production and react promptly to incidents.

### 9.4.1 Using `tracing`

The `tracing` crate offers a structured way to output logs,
which can be particularly useful in complex systems where
context is key:

```rust
use tracing::{error, info};

fn example() {

if let Err(err) = some_operation() { error!("Operation
failed: {:?}", err);

}

info!("Operation completed successfully");
```
```

```
}
```

Integrating `tracing` with an asynchronous web framework can enhance the observability of your application, leading to quicker diagnostics and repairs.

9.5 Testing Error Handling

Testing is vital to ensure your error handling logic operates as expected. You can create tests that simulate error conditions, ensuring your application responds correctly.

Using the `#[should_panic]` attribute allows you to test for panics, while Result-based functions can be tested against expected outcomes in their error handling paths.

```rust #[test]
fn test_error_handling() { let result = get_user(999);
assert!(result.is_err());

}
```

Error handling is an integral part of building resilient web applications in Rust. By leveraging the `Result` type, custom error types, and useful crates like `anyhow` and `thiserror`, developers can provide clear, manageable, and helpful error responses. Incorporating structured logging and thorough testing ensures that applications remain maintainable and reliable as they grow. As we move forward, always remember that how you handle errors can shape user experiences and the overall quality of web applications.

Managing Errors with Result and Option Types

One of the fundamental aspects of achieving safety is through its powerful type system, which includes the use of `Result` and `Option` types for managing errors and absence of values, respectively. This chapter delves into how these types can help you handle errors gracefully and efficiently.

1. Understanding the Need for Error Handling

In any programming language, error handling is a critical aspect that developers must consider. Bugs, unexpected input, and external factors can lead to runtime errors. Handling these errors appropriately ensures that the program can recover gracefully without crashing or leading to inconsistent states. In Rust, rather than relying on exceptions for error signaling, the language encourages programmers to use explicit types to handle outcomes, distinguishing between success and failure or absence of values.

2. The `Option` Type

The `Option` type in Rust represents a value that can either be `Some(T)` or `None`. This is particularly useful for situations where a value might be optional or absent. The `Option` type is defined as follows:

```rust
enum Option<T> { Some(T),
None,
}
```

2.1. Creating and Using `Option`

When a function can return a meaningful value or nothing, you can use the `Option` type:

```rust
fn find_item(id: i32) -> Option<&'static str> { let items =
vec![(1, "Item A"), (2, "Item B")]; for &(item_id, name) in
&items {
if item_id == id { return Some(name);
}
}
None
}
```

2.2. Pattern Matching with `Option`

You can handle the `Option` type using pattern matching:

```rust
match find_item(1) {
Some(item) => println!("Found: {}", item), None =>
println!("Item not found"),
}
```

Using pattern matching makes your code clear and exhaustive, as the compiler forces you to handle both cases explicitly.

3. The `Result` Type

The `Result` type is used to report the success or failure of an operation. It's defined as follows:

```rust
enum Result<T, E> { Ok(T),
Err(E),
}
```

The `Result` type is immensely useful for functions that may fail, returning a successful result (`Ok`) or an error (`Err`).

3.1. Creating and Using `Result`

Consider a function that parses an integer from a string. This operation can fail, so it makes sense to use `Result`:

```rust
fn parse_integer(input: &str) -> Result<i32, String> {
match input.parse::<i32>() {
Ok(value) => Ok(value),
Err(_) => Err("Failed to parse integer".to_string()),
}
}
```

3.2. Handling `Result`

You can use pattern matching to handle the `Result` type:

150

```rust
match parse_integer("42") {
Ok(value) => println!("Parsed value: {}", value), Err(e) =>
println!("Error: {}", e),
}
```

Alternatively, the `?` operator provides a concise way to propagate errors:

```rust
fn do_something() -> Result<(), String> {
let value = parse_integer("not a number")?;
println!("Parsed value: {}", value);
Ok(())
}
```

If an error occurs, it gets returned immediately from the function, making error handling straightforward. ## 4. Composing `Option` and `Result`

You can also compose `Option` and `Result` types to deal with functions that may have optional values and errors:

```rust
fn get_item_or_error(id: i32) -> Result<&'static str, String> { match find_item(id) {
Some(item) => Ok(item),
```

```
None => Err("Item not found".to_string()),

  }

}
```
` ` `

Using these types together allows for robust error handling flows, giving you the flexibility to manage various failure scenarios in a type-safe manner.

5. Best Practices for Error Handling in Rust ### 5.1. Use Descriptive Errors

When defining error types, use descriptive and meaningful error messages to aid debugging.

` ` `rust #[derive(Debug)] enum MyError {

```
NotFound(String), InvalidInput(String),

}

fn example_function(input:   &str)   ->   Result<i32,
MyError> { if input.is_empty() {

return   Err(MyError::InvalidInput("Input   cannot   be
empty".to_string()));

}

// Further logic...

}
```
` ` `

5.2. Consider Custom Error Types

For more complex applications, consider defining your custom error types. This will make it easier to categorize and handle different error scenarios:

````rust #[derive(Debug)] pub enum Error {
IoError(std::io::Error),
ParseError(std::num::ParseIntError),
}
impl From<std::io::Error> for Error { fn from(err: std::io::Error) -> Error {

Error::IoError(err)
}
}
impl From<std::num::ParseIntError> for Error { fn from(err: std::num::ParseIntError) -> Error {
Error::ParseError(err)
}
}
````

5.3. Use the `anyhow` crate for Quick Prototypes

For rapid development or prototyping, consider using the `anyhow` crate, which provides an easy way to handle errors without needing to define custom error types:

````rust
use anyhow::{Result, Context};

fn main() -> Result<()> {
let _ = std::fs::read_to_string("config.toml").context("Failed to
````

read config")?; Ok(())

}

\`\`\`

By providing explicit ways to represent errors and absence of values, Rust enables developers to create applications that maintain stability even in the face of unexpected conditions. Familiarity with these types and their usage will greatly enhance your ability to manage errors efficiently in your Rust applications.

Embrace these tools thoughtfully, and you'll be well on your way to building resilient software.

Implementing Custom Error Types for APIs

In this chapter, we will delve into the creation of custom error types in Rust for API development, exploring the benefits they provide in terms of clarity, control, and usability.

Understanding Rust's Error Handling Model

Rust distinguishes between two kinds of errors: recoverable and unrecoverable. Recoverable errors are typically represented through the `Result<T, E>` type, while unrecoverable errors are represented through the `panic!` macro. For API development, our primary focus is on recoverable errors since they allow for graceful handling and informative responses to the client.

The `Result` type is defined as:

\`\`\`rust

pub enum Result<T, E> { Ok(T),

154

```
Err(E),

}
```
```` ` ` ` ````

In web APIs, errors convey essential information about what went wrong during the request, making it imperative to define a robust system for error representation.

Why Custom Error Types?

While Rust provides basic error types through the standard library, creating custom error types offers significant advantages:

Clarity: Custom errors can be explicitly tied to specific API conditions, making debugging and client error handling clearer.

Extensibility: You can easily add more context, fields, or variants as your application evolves.

Interoperability: Custom errors can be serialized into a more user-friendly JSON format for API response.

Creating a Custom Error Type

Let's implement a simple custom error type for a RESTful API. We will define an `ApiError` enum encapsulating various error scenarios.

Step 1: Define the Error Enum

We will create an enum that covers various types of errors that might occur within our API.

```rust
use serde::{Deserialize, Serialize}; use std::fmt;
```
```

```rust
#[derive(Debug, Serialize, Deserialize)] pub enum
ApiError {

NotFound(String),


InvalidInput(String),              Unauthorized(String),
InternalServerError(String),
}
impl fmt::Display for ApiError {

fn fmt(&self, f: &mut fmt::Formatter<'_>) -> fmt::Result {
match self {

ApiError::NotFound(msg) => write!(f, "Not Found: {}",
msg), ApiError::InvalidInput(msg) => write!(f, "Invalid
Input: {}", msg), ApiError::Unauthorized(msg)   =>
write!(f,        "Unauthorized:        {}",        msg),
ApiError::InternalServerError(msg) => write!(f, "Internal
Server Error: {}", msg),

}
}
}
```

Step 2: Implementing `From` for Error Conversion

To make it easier to convert different error types into our
custom `ApiError`, we can implement the `From` trait.

```rust
use std::convert::From;

impl From<std::io::Error> for ApiError { fn from(err:
```

```rust
std::io::Error) -> ApiError {
    ApiError::InternalServerError(err.to_string())
    }
}
// Additional implementations can follow for other error
types as needed.
```

Step 3: Implementing Error Handling in API Endpoints

Let's demonstrate how to use the custom error type in a simple API endpoint. We will use the `warp` framework as an example, but the concepts can be applied to other frameworks like `actix-web` or `rocket`.

```rust
use warp::Filter;
#[tokio::main] async fn main() {
    let api = warp::path("items")
    .and(warp::get())
    .and_then(handle_get_items);
    warp::serve(api).run(([127, 0, 0, 1], 3030)).await;
}
async fn handle_get_items() -> Result<impl warp::Reply,
warp::Rejection> {
    // Simulate fetching items, which may produce errors
    let result: Result<Vec<String>, std::io::Error> =
```

157

```
fetch_items().await;

match result {

Ok(items) => Ok(warp::reply::json(&items)),

Err(err)                                    =>
Err(warp::reject::custom(ApiError::from(err))),

}

}

async fn fetch_items() -> Result<Vec<String>,
std::io::Error> {

// Assume some DB fetch that could fail
Err(std::io::Error::new(std::io::ErrorKind::NotFound,
"No items found"))

}
```

Step 4: Custom Error Response

To return a structured error response to the client, we'll need to implement the `warp::reject::Reject` trait for our `ApiError`.

```rust
impl warp::reject::Reject for ApiError {}

async fn handle_rejection(err: warp::Rejection) ->
Result<impl warp::Reply, warp::Rejection> { if let
Some(api_error) = err.find::<ApiError>() {

let json = warp::reply::json(&api_error);

return                 Ok(warp::reply::with_status(json,
warp::http::StatusCode::INTERNAL_SERVER_ERROR));
```

```
}
// Handle other potential rejections... Err(err)
}
```

Using the Error Handler in the API

To wire up the rejection handler with our API, we modify our main function:

```rust
let api = warp::path("items")
.and(warp::get())
.and_then(handle_get_items)
.recover(handle_rejection);
```

Custom error types in Rust not only enhance the expressiveness of error handling in APIs but also improve the API's communication with clients. By creating a well-defined error model, developers can ensure that API consumers receive meaningful feedback, aiding in debugging and enhancing user experience.

Chapter 10: Securing Web Applications

Rust, with its unique approach to memory safety and performance, has emerged as a strong contender for building robust web applications. This chapter delves into the strategies and best practices for securing web applications in Rust, offering insights into how its features can be leveraged to minimize vulnerabilities and enhance overall security.

Understanding Web Application Security

Before diving into the specifics of securing web applications in Rust, it's essential to grasp the primary threats and vulnerabilities web applications face. Common issues include:

Injection Attacks: Such as SQL injections or command injections, where an attacker sends malicious input to exploit application behavior.

Cross-Site Scripting (XSS): Occurs when an application includes untrusted data in a web page without proper validation or escaping, allowing attackers to execute scripts in users' browsers.

Cross-Site Request Forgery (CSRF): A type of attack that tricks the user into executing unwanted actions on a different site where they are authenticated.

Insecure Direct Object References: Flaws that allow attackers to gain unauthorized access to resources by modifying input data.

Sensitive Data Exposure: Poor management of sensitive data, including passwords, tokens, or personal information, which can lead to data breaches.

By understanding these potential threats, we can utilize Rust's features effectively to develop secure web applications.

Leveraging Rust Features for Security #### Memory Safety

One of Rust's most significant advantages is its emphasis on memory safety without the need for garbage collection. This allows developers to avoid common pitfalls such as null pointer dereferences and buffer overflows that can lead to security vulnerabilities. Here are a few techniques to maintain memory safety in web applications:

Ownership and Borrowing: Rust's ownership model enforces strict rules on how memory is accessed. By using ownership and borrowing effectively, we can ensure that data races and dangling references are minimized.

Immutable Data Structures: Utilizing immutable data structures whenever possible can reduce the surface for bugs and potential vulnerabilities.

Error Handling

Rust's approach to error handling—using the `Result` and `Option` types—encourages developers to handle errors gracefully. In the context of web applications, this means:

Propagating Errors: Always propagate errors to stakeholders. Instead of failing silently or crashing, provide meaningful messages while logging the details for developers.

Handling User Input: Validate and sanitize all user input to prevent possible injection attacks. Rust's type system and methods such as regex can help in validating the incoming data.

Dependency Management

Using external libraries is common in web development. Rust's package manager, Cargo, allows for secure and easy dependency management. To enhance security:

Review Dependencies: Regularly audit third-party dependencies for vulnerabilities using tools like

`cargo-audit`. Keeping dependencies up-to-date minimizes exposure to known risks.

Use Crates with Care: When choosing crates (Rust's term for packages), ensure they are well-maintained, have a strong user base, and are written with security in mind.

Best Practices for Securing Web Applications in Rust
Implementing HTTPS

Use HTTPS to encrypt communications between the client and server. Rust has several libraries, such as

`hyper` and `rustls`, that facilitate the implementation of secure protocols. #### Authentication and Authorization

Secure Password Management: Use hashing algorithms like bcrypt or Argon2 for password storage. Libraries like `bcrypt` are available in Rust for efficient password hashing.

Role-Based Access Control (RBAC): Design and implement a robust RBAC mechanism to ensure users have appropriate permissions for their actions.

Protect Against Common Vulnerabilities

Input Validation and Sanitization: Validate input thoroughly and sanitize it to prevent XSS and SQL injection attacks.

Cross-Site Request Forgery Prevention: Use cryptographic tokens like CSRF tokens to ensure that state-changing requests come from authenticated users.

Implement Rate Limiting: Prevent abuse and denial-of-service attacks by implementing rate limiting on sensitive operations.

Testing and Monitoring

Continuous testing and monitoring are critical for maintaining the security of web applications. In Rust, consider the following:

Unit Testing: Implement comprehensive unit tests to verify code functionality and behavior, particularly for modules that handle critical security functions.

Integration Testing: Carry out integration tests to ensure that components work together securely, especially those involved in user authentication and data handling.

Logging and Monitoring: Implement logging to capture suspicious activities and continuously monitor for anomalies that could indicate a security incident.

By adhering to best practices, leveraging Rust's powerful type system and memory management, and continuously monitoring and testing applications, developers can build robust, secure web applications that safeguard users' data and privacy. As the landscape of cybersecurity continues to evolve, staying informed and proactive about security measures will be crucial for any web developer in Rust.

Protecting APIs with HTTPS and SSL/TLS

With the increasing number of data breaches and cyber threats, protecting sensitive information transmitted over networks should be a top priority for developers. This chapter delves into the importance of HTTPS and Secure Sockets Layer/Transport Layer Security (SSL/TLS) protocols and how to implement them in Rust web applications.

Understanding HTTPS and SSL/TLS ### What is HTTPS?

HyperText Transfer Protocol Secure (HTTPS) is an extension of HTTP that uses encryption to secure the data transferred between a client (such as a web browser) and a server. Using HTTPS, information such as login credentials, payment details, or personal data is encrypted, ensuring that even if the data is intercepted, it cannot be easily read by unauthorized parties.

What are SSL and TLS?

SSL (Secure Sockets Layer) was the original protocol to secure internet communications. While SSL has become obsolete due to various security vulnerabilities, its successor, TLS (Transport Layer Security), is widely used today for secure communications over the internet. As we implement secure APIs in Rust, we refer to TLS when discussing secure communication.

Why Use HTTPS?

There are several reasons why securing APIs with HTTPS

is crucial:

Data Encryption: Encrypting data protects it from eavesdropping, making it unintelligible to attackers intercepting the traffic.

Data Integrity: HTTPS ensures that data transferred between the client and server hasn't been tampered with during transit.

Authentication: It helps confirm that the parties involved in the communication are who they claim to be, thus preventing man-in-the-middle attacks.

SEO Benefits: Search engines like Google favor HTTPS sites over HTTP ones, often ranking them higher in search results.

Setting Up HTTPS in Rust

To set up HTTPS in a Rust web application, you'll typically follow these steps:

Generate a Certificate and Private Key: For production environments, you should obtain a certificate from a Certificate Authority (CA). For development purposes, you can create self-signed certificates using the OpenSSL tool or other tools designed for this purpose.

```bash
# Generate a private key

openssl genrsa -out server.key 2048 # Create a self-signed certificate

openssl req -new -x509 -key server.key -out server.crt -days 365 -subj "/C=US/ST=State/L=City/O=Organization/OU=Unit/CN
```

=example.com"
```

**Adding Dependencies**: Ensure you have the necessary crates in your `Cargo.toml` file. The following example uses `hyper` for building the HTTP server and `tokio` as the runtime. You'll also need `rustls` for enabling TLS.

```toml [dependencies] hyper = "0.14"

tokio = { version = "1.0", features = ["full"] } rustls = "0.20"

tokio-rustls = "0.23"
```

Setting Up the Server: The next step is to set your server to use the generated certificate and key to accept HTTPS connections.

```rust
use hyper::{Body, Request, Response, Server}; use hyper::service::{make_service_fn, service_fn}; use tokio_rustls::TlsAcceptor;

use std::sync::{Arc, Mutex}; use std::fs::File;

use std::io::BufReader; use std::net::SocketAddr;

async fn handle_request(req: Request<Body>) -> Result<Response<Body>, hyper::Error> { Ok(Response::new(Body::from("Hello, HTTPS!")))
}

#[tokio::main] async fn main() {
// Load certificate and key
```
```

```
let              cert_file              =              &mut
BufReader::new(File::open("server.crt").unwrap());    let
key_file                    =                    &mut
BufReader::new(File::open("server.key").unwrap());    let
certs = rustls::internal::pemfile::certs(cert_file).unwrap();

let            mut            keys            =
rustls::internal::pemfile::rsa_private_keys(key_file).unwr
ap();              let              config            =
rustls::ServerConfig::new(rustls::NoClientAuth::new());

let config = Arc::new(config);

let addr = SocketAddr::from(([127, 0, 0, 1], 443));

let make_svc = make_service_fn(|_conn| async { Ok::<_,
hyper::Error>(service_fn(handle_request)) }); let server
= Server::bind(&addr)

.serve(make_svc);

let tls_acceptor = TlsAcceptor::from(config);

// Run the server

if let Err(e) = server.await { eprintln!("Server error: {}", e);
}
}
```

In this example, we set up a simple HTTP server that responds with "Hello, HTTPS!" to incoming requests while using TLS for secure communications. You need to replace `127.0.0.1` and `443` with your server's address and the port you wish to use. ## Testing Your Server

After starting your server, you can test it using tools such as `curl`:

```bash
curl -k https://localhost
```

The `-k` flag is used to ignore certificate validation issues for self-signed certificates. For production, ensure you use a certificate signed by a trusted CA.

By understanding the importance of these protocols and implementing them correctly, developers can significantly enhance the security of their web applications and protect user data from potential threats. As web development continues to evolve, embracing security best practices is crucial for building robust and trustworthy applications.

Defending Against Common Web Vulnerabilities

While many programming languages have their inherent vulnerabilities, Rust offers a unique advantage with its focus on memory safety and concurrency. This chapter delves into common web vulnerabilities and the proactive measures you can implement in Rust to defend against them.

Understanding Common Web Vulnerabilities

Before diving into defense mechanisms, it's essential to understand the common vulnerabilities that plague web applications. The Open Web Application Security Project (OWASP) maintains a widely recognized list of these vulnerabilities, which includes:

SQL Injection: Attackers can inject malicious SQL

code into queries, potentially gaining unauthorized access to databases.

Cross-Site Scripting (XSS): XSS vulnerabilities allow attackers to inject scripts into web pages viewed by other users, compromising their sessions and data.

Cross-Site Request Forgery (CSRF): This involves tricking the user's browser into making unwanted actions on a different site where they are authenticated.

Insecure Deserialization: Attackers can exploit applications that deserialize data. This could lead to remote code execution or data tampering.

Security Misconfiguration: Poor configuration in web servers, databases, or APIs can expose sensitive data.

Sensitive Data Exposure: Applications might inadvertently leak sensitive information due to improper encryption.

Leveraging Rust's Safety Features

Rust's strict compile-time checks and the absence of a garbage collector aid in building secure applications. These features can significantly mitigate common vulnerabilities.

1. Integrating Strong Typing and Ownership

SQL Injection: When building web applications, use parameterized queries, which Rust's database libraries like `Diesel` or `SQLx` support natively. By avoiding raw SQL concatenation, you inherently reduce the risk of SQL injection attacks:

```rust
```

```
sqlx::query!("SELECT * FROM users WHERE email =
$1", email)
.fetch_one(&pool)
.await?;
```

XSS: For preventing XSS, always escape user input and avoid inserting raw data into HTML. Libraries like `html_escape` can help safely handle and encode user data.

```rust
let safe_input = html_escape::encode_text(user_input);
```

2. Utilizing Secure Libraries

For WS and CSRF vulnerabilities, Rust provides a robust ecosystem of libraries aimed at fortifying web applications. For example, use `actix-web` or `warp`, which inherently support security features.

CSRF: Implement CSRF tokens that are validated on state-changing requests. The `csrf` crate provides necessary functions to generate and verify these tokens.

```rust
use csrf::{CsrfToken, CsrfStore};
let csrf = CsrfToken::new();
```

3. Regular Dependencies Audit

Rust's package manager, Cargo, allows you to track and manage dependencies effectively. Regularly audit your dependencies for vulnerabilities using `cargo audit`, which leverages the RustSec Advisory Database.

4. Proper Configuration Management

To prevent security misconfigurations, utilize environment variables for sensitive configurations (like API keys). Libraries such as `dotenv` assist in managing environment variables without hardcoding sensitive data in your source code.

```rust
dotenv::dotenv().ok();

let api_key = std::env::var("API_KEY").expect("API_KEY must be set");
```

5. Employing Secure Transport Protocols

Sensitive Data Exposure: Always use HTTPS for data transmission. The `rustls` library can facilitate configuring TLS in your Rust applications.

```rust
use rustls::ServerConfig;

// Configure your ServerConfig for secure transport
```

By leveraging Rust's strong typing, ownership model, and its array of security libraries, you can create resilient web applications that mitigate risks. As you continue to develop in Rust, remember that security is not a one-time task but an ongoing process that requires vigilance and adaptability to emerging vulnerabilities.

Chapter 11: Testing and Debugging

Rust, with its focus on safety and performance, provides a rich set of tools that facilitate effective testing and debugging. In this chapter, we'll explore the strategies and methodologies for testing and debugging Rust applications specifically tailored for web development.

11.1 The Importance of Testing

Testing is an integral part of software development. It allows developers to identify and fix bugs before they reach the end user, ensures that features work as intended, and serves as documentation for the application's functionality. In the realm of web development, where applications are dynamic and user interactions are unpredictable, having a comprehensive testing suite is vital.

11.1.1 Types of Testing

Before diving into Rust-specific testing tools, it's important to understand the different types of testing you may encounter:

Unit Testing: Testing individual components in isolation. In Rust, these are typically functions in the form of small, isolated tests that verify the logic of a specific function.

Integration Testing: Testing how different parts of the application work together. This often involves calling multiple functions or modules to ensure they interact correctly.

Functional Testing: Testing the application as a

whole, focusing on user acceptance criteria. This is often accomplished through end-to-end tests that simulate user behavior.

Performance Testing: Evaluating the performance, stability, and scalability of the application under various load conditions.

Regression Testing: Ensuring that new changes have not adversely affected existing features. ## 11.2 Setting Up Testing in Rust

Rust comes with a built-in test framework that simplifies the process of writing tests. To get started, you will need to write your tests in the same file as your code or in separate test modules and files.

11.2.1 Writing Tests

In Rust, tests are written as functions annotated with the `#[test]` attribute. Here's a simple example:

```rust
fn add(a: i32, b: i32) -> i32 { a + b
}
#[cfg(test)] mod tests {
use super::*;
```

```
#[test]
fn test_add() { assert_eq!(add(2, 3), 5);
assert_eq!(add(0, 0), 0);
assert_eq!(add(-1, 1), 0);
}
}
```

This code demonstrates a basic unit test for an `add` function. Notice how we use `#[cfg(test)]` to conditionally compile the test module only when running tests.

11.2.2 Running Tests

To run your tests, simply execute the following command in your terminal:

```bash
cargo test
```

This command will compile your code (if necessary) and run all tests found in your codebase, providing you with detailed feedback on passing and failing tests.

11.3 Integration Testing

Integration tests in Rust are stored in the `tests` directory, which Cargo expects to find at the root of your project. Here's how to create an integration test:

Create a `tests` directory.

Inside this directory, add a new file, e.g., `integration_test.rs`.

```rust
```

```
use my_crate; // Adjust this to your crate's name

#[test]

fn test_integration() {

let result = my_crate::some_function(); assert_eq!(result,
expected_value);

}
```
```

Integration tests can check the interaction between
components and ensure the entire system behaves as
expected when viewed collectively.

## 11.4 Debugging in Rust

Debugging is the process of identifying and resolving bugs
or issues within your code. Rust provides several tools and
strategies to help with debugging.

### 11.4.1 Using the `println!` Macro

In many cases, simple output statements can help track
down issues. The `println!` macro allows you to print
values and messages to the console. For example:

```rust
fn calculate(value: i32) -> i32 { println!("Calculating
value: {}", value); value * 2

}
```

11.4.2 Using Debuggers

For more complex issues, employing a debugger can be
invaluable. Rust's integration with debuggers such as

175
```

GDB and LLDB enables you to set breakpoints, inspect variables, and step through code execution. When using these tools, you'll typically need to compile your Rust program in debug mode:

```bash
cargo build --debug
```

Then, you can launch your debugger against the generated binary. ### 11.4.3 The `debug_assert!` Macro

The `debug_assert!` macro allows you to check conditions only in debug builds. This can be particularly useful for checking invariants without incurring a performance cost in release builds:

```rust
fn safe_divide(a: f64, b: f64) -> f64 { debug_assert!(b != 0.0, "Division by zero"); a / b
}
```

11.5 Error Handling in Rust

Rust's approach to error handling is distinct, utilizing the `Result` and `Option` types. When developing web applications, careful error handling is crucial, especially for user-facing applications. Handle errors gracefully and log them for debugging purposes.

11.5.1 Using `Result` and `Option`

```rust
fn fetch_data(url: &str) -> Result<Data, Error> {
```

```
// Logic to fetch data

}

match fetch_data("http://example.com") {

Ok(data) => println!("Received data: {:?}", data), Err(e)
=> eprintln!("Error fetching data: {}", e),

}
```
` ` `

In production systems, ensuring that errors are logged properly and that reasonable fallback strategies are in place will make debugging far easier if an issue occurs in production.

Testing and debugging are vital practices in the development of reliable web applications. Rust's testing framework, coupled with its rigorous approach to error handling, provides developers with the tools necessary to build robust applications. By embracing these practices, you can enhance the quality of your code, ensuring your web applications are not only performant but also resilient to failure.

Writing Unit and Integration Tests for APIs

In Rust programming, particularly when developing APIs, writing unit tests and integration tests is essential for maintaining code quality and reliability. This chapter will guide you through the processes of writing effective unit and integration tests for your APIs in Rust, providing examples to illustrate key concepts.

Understanding Rust's Testing Framework

Rust has a built-in testing framework that simplifies the development and execution of tests. You can define tests in the same file as your code or in separate modules. The Rust testing framework relies on conventions:

Unit tests are typically placed in the same file as the module they test.

Integration tests are located in the `tests` directory at the root of the project. ### Unit Tests

Unit tests are essential for validating individual components of your API, ensuring that functions and methods behave as expected. They are particularly useful for testing business logic, error handling, and edge cases without depending on external systems like databases or network calls.

Writing Unit Tests

Let's consider a simple API that includes a function to add two integers. Here's how to write a unit test for it:

```rust
// src/lib.rs
pub fn add(a: i32, b: i32) -> i32 { a + b
}
// Unit test module #[cfg(test)]
mod tests {
use super::*; // Importing the function to be tested
#[test]
```

```
fn test_add() { assert_eq!(add(2, 3), 5);
assert_eq!(add(-1, 1), 0);
assert_eq!(add(0, 0), 0);
}
#[test]
fn test_add_negative() { assert_eq!(add(-2, -3), -5);
}
}
```

In this code snippet, we define the `add` function and create a test module. The `#[cfg(test)]` attribute ensures that the test module is only compiled when tests are run. The `#[test]` attribute marks the functions as test cases. Each test case includes assertions that validate the functionality of the `add` function. #### Running Unit Tests

You can run your tests using the command line with the following command:

```bash
cargo test
```

This command compiles your code and runs all tests defined in your modules, providing output that indicates which tests passed and which failed.

Integration Tests

Integration tests validate the behavior of your entire API as a whole, testing how different components interact with each other and with external systems. They allow you to simulate real-world usage of your API and ensure that its various parts work together seamlessly.

Writing Integration Tests

To create integration tests, you generally place your test modules inside a `tests` directory at the root of your project. Each `.rs` file in this directory is compiled as a separate crate. For instance, you might create a file called `api_integration_tests.rs`.

Here's an example of an integration test for an API endpoint:

```rust
// tests/api_integration_tests.rs use reqwest;

use serde_json::Value;

#[tokio::main] async fn main() {

let                          response                       =
reqwest::get("http://localhost:8000/api/add?a=5&b=3")

.await

.expect("Failed       to       send       request");
assert_eq!(response.status(), 200);

let          json_response:          Value          =
response.json().await.expect("Failed  to  parse  JSON");
assert_eq!(json_response["result"], 8);

}
```

In this example, we use the `reqwest` crate to send a GET request to an API endpoint that sums two numbers. We assert that the response status is 200 OK and validate the contents of the returned JSON.

Running Integration Tests

Integration tests are executed similarly to unit tests using the `cargo test` command. The framework will automatically identify and run tests located within the `tests` directory.

Best Practices for Testing APIs in Rust

Test Early and Often: Write tests as you develop your API. This practice fosters a test-driven development (TDD) mindset, which helps catch bugs early and ensures that your code meets its specifications.

Use Mocking Where Appropriate: When testing API interactions, consider using libraries like

`mockito` to simulate external services and avoid hitting live endpoints during your tests.

Test Edge Cases: Ensure that your tests cover not only typical use cases but also edge cases to verify your API's robustness.

Keep Tests Isolated: Strive to maintain independence between tests. Shared state can lead to flaky tests, making it harder to determine the source of failure.

Leverage Cargo Features: Organize related tests into separate files and modules, commenting your tests clearly to describe what each one validates.

Writing unit and integration tests for APIs in Rust is an invaluable practice that enhances code reliability and maintainability. The built-in testing framework, coupled with the ability to use powerful external libraries, allows developers to create comprehensive test suites that validate the functionality of their APIs. By following the practices outlined in this chapter, you'll be able to build a robust suite of tests, thus ensuring that your Rust APIs perform as expected in real-world conditions.

Debugging and Logging Best Practices

Debugging and logging are vital components of software development, particularly in web applications where complex interactions, asynchronous tasks, and user-driven events abound. Rust, known for its performance and memory safety, comes with unique tools and practices that can help developers create more robust applications. This chapter explores the best practices for debugging and logging in Rust programming, specifically tailored to web development.

Understanding Rust's Error Handling

Rust's approach to error handling is one of its standout features. Unlike many languages that rely heavily on exceptions, Rust uses the `Result` and `Option` types to manage error states effectively.

Using Result and Option Types

Result Type: This type is used for functions that can return an error. It consists of two variants:

`Ok(T)` for successful outcomes and `Err(E)` for errors.

Option Type: This type is used when there may or may not be a value. It has two variants: `Some(T)` for a present value and `None` for absence.

Best Practice Tip: Always propagate errors using the `?` operator to maintain the context of the error. Instead of using `unwrap()`, which can cause panics, handle errors gracefully to improve stability.

```rust
fn read_file_content(path: &str) -> Result<String, std::io::Error> { let content = std::fs::read_to_string(path)?;
Ok(content)
}
```

Logging in Rust

Effective logging is crucial for monitoring the health of web applications and diagnosing issues. The Rust ecosystem offers several libraries for logging, with `log` and `env_logger` being among the most popular.

Setting Up Logging

To set up logging in a Rust application, you generally need to:

Add the dependencies in `Cargo.toml`:

```toml
[dependencies] log = "0.4"
env_logger = "0.9"
```

Initialize the logger in your main function:

```rust
fn main() { env_logger::init();
```

183

```
// Your application code here

}
```

Use the logger throughout your code:

```rust
use log::{info, warn, error};

fn process_request(request: &Request) { info!("Received request: {:?}", request);

// Processing logic here

if let Err(err) = perform_task(request) { error!("Error processing request: {:?}", err);

}

}
```

Log Levels

Rust's logging system supports different log levels, which helps filter the information being logged:

Error: For critical issues that affect functionality.

Warn: For potentially harmful situations that should be monitored.

Info: For informational messages that highlight the progress of the application.

Debug: For detailed debugging information.

Trace: For fine-grained informational events.

Best Practice Tip: Use appropriate log levels consistently for clarity. This allows users of your logs to quickly identify the severity of the messages.

Structured Logging

Structured logging can significantly enhance the quality of your logs, making them more analyzable. Instead of logging unstructured strings, consider logging structured data like JSON.

Rust's `serde` library can be paired with logging libraries to achieve structured logging:

```rust
use log::info;

use serde_json::json;

fn log_user_action(user_id: &str, action: &str) { let log_entry = json!({

"user_id": user_id, "action": action,

"timestamp": chrono::Utc::now(),

});

info!("{}", log_entry.to_string());

}
```

Debugging Techniques

While logging helps to monitor application health, debugging allows deep investigation into issues when they arise.

Using the Debugger

185

Rust supports debugging with tools like GDB and LLDB, which can be integrated with IDEs like Visual Studio Code or IntelliJ Rust. These allow setting breakpoints, stepping through code, and inspecting variables.

Utilizing `println!` for Quick Debugging

While not a permanent solution, using `println!` can provide immediate insights into code behavior. However, ensure to remove or replace these statements with logging before production deployment.

```rust
fn calculate(value: i32) -> i32 {

println!("Calculating for value: {}", value); // Temporary logging value * 2

}
```

Improving Error Messages

When errors occur, provide descriptive messages that will assist in diagnosing the problem. Avoid ambiguous errors and include relevant context, like input values or operational states.

```rust
fn parse_input(input: &str) -> Result<i32, String> {

input.parse::<i32>().map_err(|_|    format!("Failed to parse '{}' as an integer", input))

}
```

Performance Considerations

Ensure that logging does not degrade application performance, especially in production. Some best practices include:

Log only when necessary: Avoid excessive logging in performance-critical paths.

Log asynchronously: Libraries like `log4rs` can provide asynchronous logging, reducing the overhead during critical operations.

By leveraging Rust's error handling features, structured logging, and debugging tools, developers can facilitate smoother operations and quicker resolutions to issues. As best practices evolve, continually adapting and refining your logging and debugging strategies will keep your Rust applications healthy and performant.

Conclusion

In this eBook, we have traversed the exciting landscape of Rust programming, focusing on its capabilities for web development and building high-performance web applications and APIs. Throughout our journey, we explored the inherent strengths of Rust, including its memory safety, concurrency, and speed, which make it an ideal choice for modern web development.

We started by understanding the foundations of Rust, from syntax to its unique ownership model, which helps developers manage memory without the burden of manual handling. These features not only enhance program performance but also significantly reduce the risk of common bugs that plague software development, such as null pointer dereferences and data races.

Next, we delved into various frameworks and libraries that enable seamless web development in Rust. With tools like Actix, Rocket, and Warp, we discovered how to build robust, efficient, and scalable web applications that can handle real-world demands. We also covered RESTful APIs, demonstrating how to create and consume APIs effectively, ensuring your applications can communicate seamlessly with others.

Throughout this eBook, we emphasized practical examples and hands-on projects to illustrate the concepts discussed. These exercises serve as building blocks to help you cultivate your Rust skills and apply them to your own web development projects.

As you move forward in your journey to becoming a proficient Rust developer, remember to embrace the language's principles of safety and performance. With the growing demand for high-quality web applications and APIs, mastering Rust will position you at the forefront of web development, allowing you to create applications that are not only fast but also secure and reliable.

We hope this eBook has equipped you with the knowledge and confidence to embark on your Rust web development projects. The vibrant Rust community is a valuable resource, so don't hesitate to engage with others, share your experiences, and seek support as you continue to learn.

Thank you for joining us on this exploration of the Rust programming language for web development. We wish you the best of luck in your future projects and look forward to seeing the innovative applications you will create!

Biography

Jeff Stuart is a visionary writer and seasoned web developer with a passion for crafting dynamic and user-centric web applications. With years of hands-on experience in the tech industry, Jeff has mastered the art of problem-solving through code, specializing in Rust programming and cutting-edge web technologies. His expertise lies in creating efficient, scalable, and secure solutions that push the boundaries of what web applications can achieve.

As a lifelong learner and tech enthusiast, Jeff thrives on exploring the ever-evolving landscape of programming languages and frameworks. When he's not immersed in writing code or brainstorming innovative ideas, you'll find him sharing his knowledge through inspiring content that empowers others to unlock their full potential in the digital world.

Beyond his professional pursuits, Jeff enjoys exploring the art of minimalist design, reading thought-provoking books on technology and philosophy, and hiking to recharge his creative energies. His unwavering dedication to excellence and his belief in the transformative power of technology shine through in every page of his work, making this ebook a compelling guide for anyone eager to master the art of Rust programming and web development.

Glossary: Rust Programming Language for Web Development

A

Asynchronous Programming

A programming paradigm that allows multiple operations to run concurrently, improving the responsiveness of applications. Rust's async/await syntax simplifies writing asynchronous code, making it easier to handle I/O-bound operations typically common in web servers and clients.

Actix

A powerful actor framework for Rust that enables developers to build concurrent applications. Actix-web is a lightweight framework for creating web applications using Actix, known for its speed and efficiency.

--- ## B

Borrowing

A core concept in Rust that allows functions to access data without taking ownership of it. This mechanism ensures memory safety by preventing data races at compile time, a crucial aspect when developing web servers that handle multiple requests.

Backend

The server-side of an application that handles data processing, database interactions, and server logic. Rust is increasingly used for backend development due to its performance characteristics.

--- ## C

Cargo

The Rust package manager and build system that simplifies managing dependencies, building packages, and distributing Rust projects. Cargo is essential for any web development project in Rust, facilitating easy integration of libraries and tools.

Crate

A package of Rust code that can be shared and reused. Crates are the basic unit of modularity in Rust, allowing developers to leverage existing libraries for web development.

Concurrency

The ability of a program to manage multiple tasks simultaneously. Rust's ownership model and thread safety make it a strong candidate for building concurrent web applications.

--- ## D

Database Migration

The process of moving and transforming data between different databases or database structures. In Rust web development, tools like Diesel and SeaORM help manage migrations effectively.

Diesel

A powerful ORM (Object-Relational Mapping) library for Rust that provides a type-safe way to interact with databases. It is particularly compatible with PostgreSQL,

SQLite, and MySQL, helping to streamline database operations in web applications.

--- ## E

Error Handling

The process of responding to and managing errors in a program. Rust's error handling is done through

`Result` and `Option` types, which help developers write more reliable web applications by explicitly managing potential errors.

F

Framework

A set of reusable components and guidelines for building applications. In web development with Rust, popular frameworks include Actix-web and Rocket, each providing different tools and abstractions for building web applications.

--- ## G

GitHub

A web-based platform for version control utilizing Git. Many Rust projects, including libraries and web applications, are hosted on GitHub, facilitating collaboration and open-source contributions.

--- ## H

Hyper

A fast and low-level HTTP implementation in Rust. It serves as the foundation for many web frameworks and applications, enabling developers to create efficient web services with full control over the HTTP protocol.

--- ## I

Integrated Development Environment (IDE)

Software that provides comprehensive facilities for software development, including code editing, debugging, and build automation. Popular IDEs for Rust development include Visual Studio Code with Rust extensions and IntelliJ Rust.

--- ## J

JSON (JavaScript Object Notation)

A lightweight data interchange format that is easy for humans to read and write, and easy for machines to parse and generate. JSON is commonly used in web APIs, and Rust provides libraries like Serde for easily encoding and decoding JSON data.

--- ## K

Keep-Alive

A feature of HTTP/1.1 that allows a single TCP connection to remain open for multiple requests and responses, improving connection efficiency. Rust's libraries typically support keep-alive connections to enhance web application performance.

--- ## L

Lifetimes

A Rust feature that ensures references are valid as long as they are needed, preventing dangling references. Understanding lifetimes is crucial for developing safe backend applications in Rust, especially when handling concurrent requests.

--- ## M

Macro

A way to write code that writes other code (metaprogramming) in Rust. Macros enhance productivity and code readability, particularly when building repetitive structures common in web application frameworks.

--- ## N

Networking

The practice of connecting computers and systems to share resources and data. Rust offers excellent support for networking protocols, making it suitable for building web servers and clients.

--- ## O

Ownership

A key feature of Rust that governs how memory is managed. Every piece of data has a single owner, which ensures memory safety and prevents resource leaks, critical in web server environments.

--- ## P

PostgreSQL

An open-source relational database management system widely used in web applications. Rust developers often use libraries like Diesel to interact with PostgreSQL databases easily.

--- ## Q

Query Language

A language used to make queries on databases. In Rust, libraries like Diesel provide a type-safe query language that enhances database interactions.

--- ## R

Rocket

A web framework for Rust that simplifies the process of building fast, secure web applications. It offers a user-friendly API and extensive features to streamline web development.

--- ## S

Serde

A widely-used serialization/deserialization library in Rust that enables efficient data interchange formats like JSON, TOML, and more, commonly used in web APIs.

State Management

The process of managing the state of an application. State management is crucial in web development, especially when building web applications that require user sessions and data persistence.

--- ## T

Tokio

An asynchronous runtime for Rust that enables writing non-blocking applications. It is essential for building performant web services in Rust, particularly when dealing with high concurrency.

--- ## U

Unit Test

A level of software testing where individual components of the software are tested in isolation. Rust's built- in testing framework allows developers to write unit tests that validate the functionality of web application components.

--- ## V

Vector

A growable array type in Rust, commonly used for collecting data. In web development, vectors can be utilized to manage lists of items such as database records or API responses.

W

WebAssembly (Wasm)

A binary instruction format that allows executing code on web browsers. Rust can compile to WebAssembly, enabling developers to run performance-critical code in web interfaces efficiently.

Web Server

A software program that serves HTTP requests from clients. Rust is used to create efficient web servers, such as those built with Actix-web or Rocket.

--- ## X

XSS (Cross-Site Scripting)

A common security vulnerability that allows attackers to inject malicious scripts into web pages viewed by users. Rust's strong type system and memory safety features help minimize such vulnerabilities.

--- ## Y

YAML (YAML Ain't Markup Language)

A human-readable data serialization format. It is often used for configuration files in web applications. Rust libraries like Serde provide support for YAML, facilitating easy integration.

--- ## Z

Zero-Cost Abstractions

A principle in Rust that ensures features of the language do not impose runtime overhead. This concept is significant for web development, where performance is key.

www.ingramcontent.com/pod-product-compliance
Lightning Source LLC
LaVergne TN
LVHW051331050326
832903LV00031B/3471